YOUR LIFE PATH

LIFE MAPPING TOOLS TO HELP YOU FOLLOW YOUR HEART AND LIVE YOUR DREAM, NOW!

DR. LINDA K. WATTS

CARREL BOOKS

Carrel Books may be purchased in bulk at special discounts for sales promotion, corporate gifts, fund-raising, or educational purposes. Special editions can also be created to specifications. For details, contact the Special Sales Department, Carrel Books, 307 West 36th Street, 11th Floor, New York, NY 10018 or carrelbooks@skyhorsepublishing.com.

Carrel Books® is a registered trademark of Skyhorse Publishing, Inc.®, a Delaware corporation.

Visit our website at www.carrelbooks.com.

10 9 8 7 6 5 4 3 2 1

Library of Congress Cataloging-in-Publication Data is available on file.

Cover design by Rain Saukas
Cover photo credit: iStock

Interior chart graphics by Hwesta

Print ISBN: 978-1-63144-078-6
Ebook ISBN: 978-1-63144-079-3

Printed in the United States of America

Note to Readers: This publication is designed to provide accurate and authoritative information with respect to the subject matter covered. It is sold with the understanding that the publisher and author are not engaged in rendering psychological, financial, legal, or other professional services. If expert assistance or counseling is needed, the services of a competent professional should be sought.

Dedication

I dedicate this book to my dear mother,
Elizabeth Anne Rugh Watts.

Acknowledgments

I am grateful to my family and friends who have inspired me and to students and workshop participants whom I have learned from through their own life-mapping journeys. I especially wish to thank Linda Langton (Super-Agent), Paula Kalamaras & Paul Kraly (Scribes Unlimited), Gianmichele Grittani (Hwesta Graphics), Zvia Bird, Debra J. Breazzano, Denise Naughton, Rev. Lee Ireland, Cheryl Watts, Sophia Watts, Sri Harold Klemp, Kathleen Ulrich, Janet Parker, Corinne Harmon, Margo Stuart, and Carole and Graham Poulter, and Kery Colvin, without whose helpful reviews and heartful support this book would not have been possible.

CONTENTS

INTRODUCTION

What do you want to be or do "when you grow up?" Wherever you are in your life right now and whatever your age, you have many pathways open before you. You have the freedom to choose which future options to explore and which to leave behind.

Life Path Mapping is a self-discovery process that can help you to follow your heart every step of YOUR way forward. The credo and intended result of the self-discovery process provided with this book is for you to Live Your Dream, Now! You do not need to wait for some nebulous set of life conditions to come about such as relocation, retirement, or an empty nest. You can begin Now to implement behaviors and attitudes that allow you to create around you the life of your dreams, fulfilling your deepest values and enhancing your quality of life.

How to Use This Book

This book provides a complete Life Path Mapping guidebook with its embedded self-discovery Toolkit. The chapters will conduct you through your own life-mapping process as you compose your own Life Path Maps Portfolio using the *Tools* (journaling prompts, charting techniques, and creative representation activities) that I have provided for you at the end of each chapter. You can use a large-sized journal or sketch pad to create your Portfolio, following the directions provided for each *Tool* in this book. If you prefer, upload and print the separate *Life Path Maps Portfolio Toolkit* online for a small fee from my website, Better Endings for Your Life Path (betterendingsnow.com).

The Life Path Mapping process provided with this book proceeds through three stages as a self-discovery adventure. Each chapter-ending *Tool* fits within a gradually unfolding, layered sequence of activities and reflections designed to equip you fully to *Live Your Dream, Now!* Chapter 1 describes these three stages in detail.

Because this book conducts you through a comprehensive Life Path Mapping process, it is most useful for you to engage with the chapter-ending *Tools* sequentially. In every chapter, after I have presented a specific step or topic, text boxes will direct you to pause your reading so you can engage with a *Tool*, numbered at the end of the chapter, before you continue to read ahead. This allows you to arrive at your own personal insights before reading stories about other people's results with these *Tools*.

Although this book serves as a guide for you to compose your own Life Path Maps Portfolio on your own, you could also choose to share it and engage with the *Tools* within a study group or workshop setting. Individuals can then share insights with one another as you move through the *Tools* together.

Chapter 1

LIFE IS . . . YOUR GOLDEN OPPORTUNITY

This book is your alchemist's chemical lab. In it, may you find all the elements you need to forge a lifetime of golden fulfillment. You will distill these elements from your own life history as you have already lived it so far. So, what is your Life Dream? Do you remember it still, or have you allowed it to fade in the process of maintaining your everyday routines? Was it a fantasy then or does it inspire you still, calling out from the subtitle of this book: *Live Your Dream, Now!*?

People tend to regard their lives as uncharted territory. Thought of this way, there may be surprises—some good, others not so good—around every bend, every turn in the Road of Life. We arrive where our momentary choices or plans might land us, and when the unexpected happens, we "thank our lucky stars," or trust, to karma, or we learn to "deal with it." "That's life!" we might say. When we chart a future course at all, we usually aim to accomplish a specific goal, like how to earn a degree or what job to apply for; or you might plan for a wedding or a family vacation.

But have you ever thought of charting the course that has brought you to where you are today? Have you looked back at those bends in the road, the surprising upheavals or upturns of opportunity, with an eye for reconstructing how your own choices, beliefs, and attitudes—in connection with external circumstances—have influenced these broad brushstrokes of fate or fortune? Why should we accept that our lives remain essentially uncharted territory in the first place?

When we strike out on a journey toward a specific destination or on a lark to travel spontaneously through counties, states, or countries, we rely on maps—and nowadays satellites—to guide our progress and provide a sense of direction, however flexible, that can lead us to our desired location or to rest points along the way. Most would agree this helps us avoid the otherwise many frustrations and pitfalls of traveling blindly and, at the very least, maps afford us the capacity to arrive at our destination more quickly and smoothly. While the journey itself may still remain the destination in the sense that we wish to enjoy the ride for all its unpredictably beautiful vistas and unforeseen opportunities, still a smoother, less troublesome adventure is usually more desirable—and generally less costly in all respects—than not.

Life Path Mapping is a creative and practical toolkit that can help you arrive at your most desirable life destinations, attain your personal goals, and fulfill your most cherished Life Dream. Like a modern-day GPS device rather than a two-dimensional paper travel map, this self-discovery toolkit can help you situate your current life position in relation to a more comprehensive vantage point so you can view your past choices and attitudes, your present circumstances and intentions, and your future goals and aspirations within a holistic frame of reference. Mapping your Life Path equips you with an overview of where you are currently, where you've come from, and where you are headed that will allow you to make necessary or desirable changes of course to help you redirect or enhance your life's journey.

Some eighteen years ago, I hit a wall in my own life journey. I thought of it then as a midlife crisis. Well en route toward tenure as a professor, privately I suffered from a deep inner conflict. Should I remain at the university to continue a standard research and teaching career, putting aside lifelong ambitions for a creative writing vocation and some form of public service? I felt I might need to resign rather than accept such a compromise.

So, I started dreaming. For several months, I paid close attention to my nightly dreams and reflected on the most significant ones in a dream journal. Then one morning, clarity came. In bold, black letters emblazoned on a white sign placard set squarely between my eyes as I was waking, I read the following message:

> ## YOU HAVE THE RESPONSIBILITY
> ## TO REALIZE YOUR DREAMS,
> ## NOT JUST FOR GETTING BY.

This literal wake-up call put my midlife crisis into clear perspective. I recognize it now as a basic life credo that can apply to anyone. You, too, are responsible for doing more than just getting by. Indeed, this is more than a responsibility. It is a golden ticket: a fresh opportunity to reorient your life in accordance with your innermost strengths, values, and goals.

The understanding that I am responsible—and thereby I have a golden opportunity to realize my dreams—really hit home for me. With this new awareness emblazoned in my consciousness, over the next year I published an academic book, obtained tenure, and completed a manuscript for a science fiction novel. Six months later, I was eligible for sabbatical leave. I knew I wanted to shift the direction of my research and writing to include a public focus; but, how? Once again, I turned to my dreams for inner guidance. One morning, I woke to another direct, unavoidable message. This time I heard a gentle inner voice speaking into my right ear: "Life Paths." I had no idea at first what this phrase might even mean, but I knew instinctively it was the direction I needed to follow to engage in sabbatical research.

In 2001, I embarked upon over a decadelong study of Life Paths. From the start, I developed a basic method for charting significant Shaping Events of a person's life in a visual, graphic format. This allows people to discover themes and patterns of experience that have dominated or punctuated their lives.

Remember Socrates's famous injunction to "Know Thyself?" The first thirty persons for whom I constructed Life Maps during my sabbatical study—followed by more than five hundred others since—have told me they find the creative activity of mapping their life's journey to be a fun exercise in reviewing their past that illuminates meaningful patterns. Many say they have come to better appreciate how they have overcome challenging obstacles in their lives. Through even their most difficult experiences, they see how they have developed personal strengths for managing life's choices and transitions.

Sara (please note: all names used with the case stories in this book are fictional) told me she felt more optimistic after completing her life-mapping process. She was hesitant at first because she did not want to revisit abusive events she was subjected to as a child. Making a collage in which Sara assembled images representing her past, current, and desirable future conditions within a holistic perspective helped Sara realize she could transcend her childhood traumas by taking their lessons—not just their "lesions"—with her into a more confident future.

Over the past fifteen years, I have developed and tested the life-mapping *Tools* that this book makes available for you to engage with as a self-discovery, personal growth, and development process. With life mapping, you can revitalize or claim and then establish a realistic, practical course of action to fully realize your Life Dream.

As you engage with the activity *Tools* provided at the end of each chapter, proceeding as the text boxes within the chapters recommend, you will gradually compose your own Life Path Maps Portfolio filled with color-coded maps, reflective journal entries, picture collages, and mandala images. By completing these *Tools*, you will proceed through three self-paced stages of your personal life-mapping adventure. With chapters 1 and 2 *Tools* you will learn about how your current Life Metaphor might be influencing your outlook, and you will discover how recurring Life Themes form distinctive threads that weave the very texture and fabric of your Life Path. Chapter 3 *Tools* will reveal your own dramatic Life Story plotline in which you are the heroic protagonist, and chapter 4 *Tools* allow you to meet and greet your very own ensemble cast of mythic Archetype characters!

This book's self-discovery *Tools* can empower you to celebrate your own dynamic, unique Life Story. That you can and will be able to *Live Your Dream, Now!* is the accomplishment I fully expect you to achieve from completing your personal adventure with this book's life-mapping toolkit. Your Life Dream may be as large or small as you define it—it could be a concrete career goal or an ideal set of personal qualities and values you simply wish to embrace more fully every day. Either way, with maps in hand and the enforcement of regular checkpoints to take stock of your gradual progress, you will emerge from this adventure fully equipped to reach and surpass the destination of your innermost goals.

In addition to Socrates's call to *"Know Thyself!"* he had a great follow-up tagline: *"The unexamined life is not worth living."*

To realize your dreams instead of just getting by is to manifest a life worth living, yes? This book's embedded life-mapping *Tools* provide a set of lenses through which you can explore your Life Path to discover where you stand in relation to fulfilling your life's purpose and achieving your personal goals.

Life Metaphors You Live By

Now, let's get you started.

Is life a Road to Glory or a demolition course? Is it a slow, inevitable march into oblivion or repeating cycles of opportunity that lift you by trials and gradual achievement toward increasingly more lofty goals? To the point of this book, as you set out on your personal life-mapping journey, will you be able to switch horses midstream if you need to, transmuting lead into gold? Yes, you can!

The use of mixed metaphors is intentional here. Language is rich in colorful images that evoke qualities of a human life. When I started researching Life Paths, I set out first to explore Life Metaphors. When I asked, "What is a human lifetime like?" I wondered how people would typically reply. Would all of their metaphors reflect one same basic image, like Life is a Journey (e.g., *a Winding Road, an Adventure, a Quest*)? Or rather, would people's images of what a lifetime is like reflect conditions and trends active in their own lives at the time?

> Complete **Chapter 1**, *Tools #I:1–3* before continuing.
> (What, to you, is a human lifetime like?)

My one universal image hypothesis definitely did not bear out. People expressed a wide range of colorful Life Metaphor images that represent around ten common ideas. These included: Nature metaphors (e.g., *Life is like a Mountain* or *a Stream* or *Weather cycles*), Vehicle-in-Motion images (e.g., *Life is like a Train* or *an Ocean Liner*), up-and-down images (e.g., *Life is a Roller Coaster*), a variety of Journey motifs, Brief Spans of Time images (e.g., *Life is "a drop in the bucket"* or *"a flash in the pan"*), Story images (e.g., *a Novel*), object-oriented images (e.g., *Life is a Ladder* or *a Chain*), and chance-oriented images (e.g., *Life is a Gambling Machine*, a *puzzle*, or a *Game Board*).

To consider whether this wide variety of Life Metaphor images reflected real conditions that were active in people's lives at the time they expressed them, I developed the simple, visual life-mapping approach you can engage with yourself using chapter 2 *Tools*. Chapter 2 guides you step-by-step to visually compose your own Life Themes Map that will illuminate patterns involving your most significant, Shaping Event memories.

I have found that Life Metaphor images generally do reflect patterns of experience that are evident in how people map out the Shaping Events and the dominant Themes of their lives. For example, Scott answered my question, "What is a human lifetime like?" by expressing two Life Metaphor images. "It starts slow and speeds up," was Scott's initial response. He also told me twice during his life-mapping sessions, "They ought to give me a PhD in the *Hard Knocks of Life*."

Take a look at Scott's Life Story Map, shown below. (You will arrive at this level of life mapping by the end of chapter 3.) To read this map, notice first the clip art image icons in the key below the map and on Scott's map itself. These symbolic icons represent when the Life Themes Scott discovered by mapping some of his most significant memories—indicated by the textured and shaded lines on Scott's map—have been prominent in terms of their positive (charted above the neutral Age Line) and/or negative (charted below the neutral Age Line) impacts throughout his life.

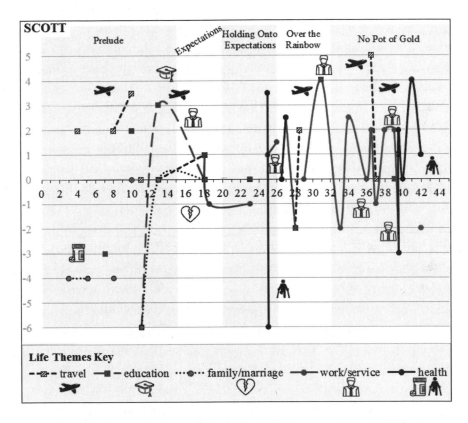

The differently textured and shaded lines on Scott's Life Story Map track the trends that these Life Themes have woven through his life. Also notice how the captions written across the top of Scott's map (i.e., *Prelude, Expectations, Holding Onto Expectations, Over the Rainbow,* and *No Pot of Gold*) are Life Chapter titles Scott used to describe phases of his life experience that have occurred between events he identified as major Turning Points.

Scott's Life Metaphor of *"Life starts slow and speeds up"* coincides with the trends that are obvious in his map even though Scott expressed this metaphor before he composed his map. Notice how the Shaping Events Scott represents on his map were few and far between in his life until he was twenty-five, after which the frequency of Scott's most memorable events and critical Turning Points certainly does appear to have "sped up." Scott was involved in a car accident when he was twenty-five from which he injured his back, and this affected his health for several years. *Health* as well as several other of Scott's Life Themes picked up momentum from that time forward.

Scott's Life Story Map reveals extremely oscillating Ups and Downs for almost all of his Life Themes. Scott's Theme of *Work/Service*, in particular, has taken Scott on a roller coaster sort of ride. Scott went through several years, since the age of twenty-seven, during which he would take a job, lose it, get a new job, and lose that one, too. Scott relocated twice (see his *Travel* Theme at the bottom of the map), hoping to "jump start" his work life and establish a more stable career. He made two major moves, first to a different city in his home state and then to California, both times to take promising sales clerk jobs. Scott had some initial success with those positions. Yet he lost each job soon after starting it; he was laid off from the first job due to downsizing, and he lost the second one because the company closed down. Both times after losing his job, Scott moved back to live with his parents. He told me that with each return to home base he increasingly resorted to drinking and partying to cope with his growing sense of personal failure.

The patterns of impact Scott associates with his Life Themes of *Family/Marriage*, *Work/Service*, and *Health*-related events reflect the second Life Metaphor image he expressed of Life as a challenging course of *Hard Knocks*. Scott's chronological sequence of Life Chapter titles dramatically conveys this *Hard Knocks* perspective. Scott sees himself as having moved through his career trials from *Expectations* to *Holding Onto Expectations* and then to striving for higher achievement with his bold move *Over the Rainbow* to

California, only to eventually come to grips with the fact that, so far, he had attained *No Pot of Gold*.

Next, meet Will, a retired pastor. As you can see from Will's Life Story Map shown below, he has charted a radically different life course than Scott's.

Will named two major life acts (bigger to him than Life Chapters): *Before Confirmation* and *After Confirmation* in the United Church of Christ. Will committed to this denomination in his teens, choosing it over a Lutheran congregation that was strong in his family and community.

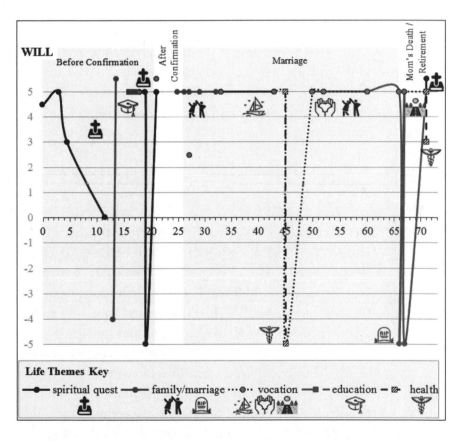

Will's Life Story Map retraces what he described as a well-blessed life. After confirmation and graduation from a theological seminary, Will enjoyed a successful vocation as a pastor. He married his high school sweetheart Paula, his true soul mate and mother of their two successful, loving sons.

Will scaled the impacts of most of his Shaping Events, for all of his five Life Themes, as extremely positive for most of the events he represents on his map. However, Will's map also records a few brief and widely separated, yet intense, bouts with depression and inner reflection. These appear on Will's map as low dips. Will described these "troughs" as periods of "deep descent" and "soul-searching." After a diagnosis of diabetes when he was forty-five, for instance, Will had a profound realization that led him to shift his career from congregational service to pastoral counseling. Later times of Descent occurred after the death of his mother and with his decision to retire. Will regards these deeply challenging times in retrospect, though, as positive opportunities that always brought him to greater degrees of clarity and self-realization.

Will expressed a fascinating Life Metaphor of *Life is a Golden Spiral*:

Will: When I close my eyes I see a linear . . . a line, but then I see a spiral.

LW: Any other details?

Will: It has molecules all around. Think of it as a wire that's coiling. It's more conical in shape than cylindrical. Along the way are little knobs or molecules that represent some highs and lows. They are significant, whatever they represent. . . . The fact that it is shaped like a cone rather than a cylinder and that it is going up suggests to me that it is like an arrow. It's pointing. It's moving toward a destination, toward a sense of fulfillment; but I don't think, at least not in this life is that achieved. It is always a process of Becoming. It is obviously going someplace.

Will offered an additional metaphor about where he sees himself in life since retiring: "I perceive myself now as sailing on the open sea, sails unfurled and filled with gentle breezes—no longer swift winds—in a process of learning to enjoy this new stage of the journey." This paints such a more positive, optimistic outlook on life than Scott's *Hard Knocks!*

Scott's and Will's mapping of the impacts of their Shaping Events and their radically different sequences of Life Chapter titles throw light on how Life Metaphors, once framed in a person's mind, can become self-reinforcing postulates. *Life is Hard Knocks*, Scott figures after a divorce and again after losing a job, and lo, his harshly Up-and-Down Life Path pattern of *Hard Knocks* continues. By contrast, Will's optimistic, spiritually motivated outlook appears to function for him like a Midas's touch that converts every critical downturn in his life into a golden opportunity for greater personal growth and development.

Life Metaphors can reinforce our attitudes and perpetuate our beliefs. That is why it may be helpful to consider how the metaphors you hold could influence how you "see things." Nevertheless, also bear in mind that as your life experience shifts in relation to your choices and attitudes, either gradually or sometimes even rather suddenly, so might your Life Metaphor image!

Are you familiar with the Indian parable of "The Six Blind Sages and the Elephant"? Each blind Indian sage, one at a time, approaches and touches the same elephant and then provides an account based on his or her perceptions of what indeed an elephant is like. One touches the trunk of the elephant and confidently declares: "An elephant is certainly like a rope!" Another blind sage touches the ear of the elephant and disagrees with the former sage's conclusions, correcting: "An elephant is actually like a fan!" So, what is the moral of this story for us here? I like to say the message of this parable is that if you were to combine all six accounts of the elephant from the six blind sages, you would wind up with a composite picture of a very funny-looking elephant! The same is true of Life Metaphors. Life Metaphors do not combine to form one overarching image or model. They reflect distinct vantage points, each equally valid depending on the life experience of the observer.

What is Your Life Course Schema?

> Complete **Chapter 1**, *Tool #I:4* before continuing. (What, to you, are the typical stages or phases, if any, of a normal human lifetime, whether or not they are typical of yours?)

Now then, consider the following three descriptive statements about life. Which of these statements comes nearest to expressing your own current understanding about how life typically is organized over time? If more than one of these statements seem valid to you, then see if you can rank order them, with #1 being the view you hold primarily right now. Record your ranking and journal about your personal viewpoint regarding these perspectives with *Tool #I:5*.

- Life advances according to a fixed order of stages.
- Life experience repeats by phases that occur naturally in periodic cycles.
- Life experiences are unpredictable and appear to be mostly random or they are often chaotic.

The three viewpoints above express three distinct mind-set orientations or cognitive "Schemas" for comprehending and experiencing life as a whole. I call these three Life Course Schema models, respectively: Linear, Cyclic, and Seamless. These three Life Course Schemas coexist and overlap within our contemporary Western cultural outlook.

Similarly as for Life Metaphors, Life Course Schemas function as internalized mind-sets that can have a profound, filtering sort of effect on how we interpret and respond to life events. You are likely to frame your day-to-day life and even your understanding of your life course overall according to one of these three Life Course Schema models as if its conceptions are naturally correct.

What if your current Life Metaphor image or your Life Course Schema predisposes you to interpret events according to a pessimistic outlook? This is where it can be useful for you to examine these internalized mental models, to consider how helpful or not they really are for you.

If you assume that life unfolds according to a fixed, linear series of stages, for instance, then if you happen to experience a divorce or you lose your job in midlife, you might feel as if you have "hit a roadblock" or you could feel "stuck" within a "midlife crisis." If you believe, instead, that life shifts cyclically every decade or so, then you may be more likely to interpret a major life experience like a divorce or a layoff as the end of one cycle and the beginning of a new cycle with refreshing, new opportunities. If you tend to think of life as being seamless, without any fixed stages or cycles, then whatever happens you might feel you can take it in stride, even though it might seem difficult for you to plan or to predict your next step.

Several other authors, including Mary Catherine Bateson in her book *Full Circles, Overlapping Lives* (Random House, 2000) and Frederic Hudson in *The Adult Years: Mastering the Art of Self-Renewal* (John Wiley & Sons, 2009), have commented on a growing tension between Linear (stage-by-stage) and Cyclical models for our contemporary lives; my own research validates these observations. The Seamless model that many people have also expressed to me contrasts distinctively with both of these other two common mind-sets.

Chapter 3 *Tools* will guide you to map and to illuminate the structure of your own Life Story. There, you may discover how your current, primary Life Metaphor image and your basic Life Course Schema model could be influencing how you conceptualize your own Shaping Events and the Life Chapters you have forged in your life up to Now.

A Bird's-Eye View of Your Life-Mapping Odyssey

This book provides the conceptual background, case stories, and a process-based sequence of self-discovery *Tools* to conduct you through your own complete Life Path Mapping adventure. You will find instructions for completing the *Tools* referred to in text boxes throughout each chapter listed at the ends of the chapters. Completing these mapping, journal reflection, and creative representation *Tools* will allow you to gradually compose your individualized Life Path Maps Portfolio.

I recommend for you to read the book chapters sequentially and engage with the chapter-ending *Tools* according to the order in which they are introduced within the chapters, pausing your reading as directed so that you will engage with the *Tool* prompts and creative activities as a gradual process. As mentioned in the introduction, I encourage you to create your own large-sized journal, perhaps with sketch paper along with some graph paper for composing your life-mapping charts, so you can gradually compose your personalized Life Path Maps Portfolio. If you prefer to download and print the *Life Path Maps Portfolio Toolkit,* you can order the author's ready-made *Tool* templates at betterendingsnow.com.

This book's chapter-ending *Tools* will conduct you through an organized sequence of self-discovery activities so that you will complete a comprehensive *rites of passage*-based life-mapping process. A rites-of-passage process is a sequence of meaningful, sometimes challenging ordeals or encounters that a person or a group of people might undergo together in order to bring about a positive, meaningful life transition, which can bring about a fundamental transformation of perspective, behavior, and consciousness. The life-mapping procedures provided with this book's *Tools* conduct you through the three recognized universal stages of a Rites-of-Passage Cycle. The outline below presents a bird's-eye view of these three primary rites-of-passage stages as they correspond with this book's self-discovery *Tools*.

STAGE ONE: Your *Separation* Process (Chapters 1–3)
With Stage One you will be taking time apart from your everyday routines to reflect on your Life Path by identifying and reflecting on your Shaping Events, critical Turning Points, Life Themes, and the

meaningful Life Chapters of your unique Life Story so far. You will discover how your Life Story compares with classic myths or popular story lines, with you as the heroic protagonist of a unique and dramatic story.

STAGE TWO: **Your** *Transformation* **Process (Chapters 4–6)**
Stage Two of your life-mapping adventure allows you to illuminate and reflect deeply upon patterns and trends that have already occurred in your Life Story. You will discover where you are, how you have gotten here, and where it is you desire to go from here. The chapter-ending *Tools* and creative activities will help you to reflect upon and better understand how you have already weathered major life transitions and how you have gained important Life Lessons through the opportunities and challenges of your Life Story to now.

In this central *Transformation* stage of your personal rites-of-passage adventure, you are invited to meet and greet your own ensemble cast of mythic Archetype characters, similarly as Dorothy encounters in *The Wizard of Oz*. These are "parts of Self" that are intrinsic to your full personality makeup, based on twelve universal Archetype figures recognized in archetypal psychology.

Innovative techniques including a seven-step Archetype Dialogue Practice that you can begin to engage with during this *Transformation* stage equips you to meet and greet your own Life Theme-related "persona Archetypes" and to discover their influence in your everyday life choices and attitudes.

For those of you who might feel reluctant to entertain the notion of "unconscious Archetypes,"—as not everyone is comfortable with this approach depending on your background or your beliefs—you will have the option to reflect instead on personal character qualities that you associate with your self-identified, situational Life Themes as these relate to your everyday social roles.

Chapter 6 *Tools* invite you to engage with a set of creative activities that will help you to "excavate" and lay claim to your personally meaningful Life Dream. You can then begin to envision qualities or conditions you wish to manifest in your most desirable Future Life Path scenario.

STAGE THREE: Your *Reintegration* Process (Chapters 7–9)

Completing your *Tools* activities through chapter 6 prepares you to "Set Your Course, and Go!" Stage Three of your life-mapping rites-of-passage adventure provides you with a set of fun, creative "totemic representation" *Tools*. These *Tools* can help you to effectively ground your newly gained insights with personally meaningful artistic representations including a pictorial collage and your own Life Dream Mandala. These artistic reminders will help you to focus your intentions as you set forth to *Live Your Dream, Now!*

Altogether, the life-mapping toolkit embedded throughout this book via the chapter-ending *Tools* fully equips you with techniques and activities that let you envision and bring about desirable life conditions so you will realize your highest ambitions and fulfill your greatest potentials! In the process, you will gain many insights about your personal character values and your Strengths that will empower you to transform self-limiting attitudes while manifesting the life of your dreams.

Poised in the Present, regardless of how we have arrived Here, we are all Threshold Dwellers in terms used by the well-known comparative and personal mythologist Joseph Campbell in his popular book, *The Hero with a Thousand Faces* (New World Library, [1949]/2008). Campbell invoked for each of us to "Take the Journey," which he liked to refer to as "the High Adventure of the Soul"—that is, to actively "Follow Your Bliss." In a similar vein, this book's *Tools* and its credo of *Live Your Dream, Now!* empowers you to actively manifest your Bliss.

Since I have mentioned the master mythologist Joseph Campbell, it feels only proper for me to close this opening chapter of *Your Life Path* with a caveat Campbell himself would likely remind you of at this significant stepping-off point. Crossing the Threshold to embark upon your personal odyssey of self-discovery so you can claim and then realize your Life Dream will require more from you than blindly stepping forward. What lurks beyond those dark gates, what Threshold Guardians may lie in wait to beset your progress? Without a clear understanding of your personal Life Mission or purpose and without a deep appreciation of your own heroic character traits to aid you in defining at least the broad parameters of your Quest, how can you realistically expect the future to be any more than an extension of the perpetual "present" threshold you find yourself standing at today?

The Quest you can realistically aim to fulfill with this book's *Tools* requires more from you than Just Getting By. The Life Dream you envision and begin to *Live Now*! is one that will benefit not only yourself but your entire world and all those you love and serve. Completing this book's *Tools* can equip you with a vessel of your own making that you can use to effectively Cross the Threshold to new dimensions of your own Life Path, grounded in a more holistically integrated Self.

Complete **Chapter 1,** *Tools #I:5–9* before continuing.

I invite you to embark and to enjoy your Journey!

Chapter 1 *TOOLS*

Your Life Path Portfolio

I:1 My Life Metaphor
Journal: What, to you, is a human lifetime like? Close your eyes to imagine a lifetime; what picture, idea, or image comes to your mind?

I:2 My Life Metaphor description
Journal: Describe or explain IN WHAT WAYS is a human lifetime like the image you have expressed for *Tool #I:1*?

I:3 Picturing My Life Metaphor
Create: Find a magazine or a computer image, or compose a collage of images, or create your own artistic image to represent your Life Metaphor from *Tool #I:1*.

I:4 My Life Course Schema model
Journal: What, to you, are the typical stages or phases—if any—of a normal human lifetime, whether or not they are typical of yours?

I:5 Rank order (number #1-#3 in your *Life Path Maps Portfolio*) the following Life Course Schema statements, according to their relevance to your own life experience. Then journal about how this understanding has been important in your life:

Life advances according to a definite, fixed order of stages.
Life repeats phases occurring in periodic cycles.
Life experiences appear mostly random or they are often chaotic.

I:6 My Origin Story
Journal: A Life Story begins with an Origin Tale. What is yours? Journal on the lines below your response to the following prompt:

I Am Who I Am Today Because . . .

I:7 A) My Vision Quest
Journal: A meaningful rites-of-passage adventure begins with a Vision Quest. Journal your responses to the following prompt:

When I Grow Up I Want to Be . . .

Then (As I might have answered this question during child-hood); and **Now** (As I would answer this question today)

I:7 B) My Vision Quest. (When I Grow Up I Want to Be . . .)
Journal: In what ways does your answer to this prompt today resemble or differ from how you might have answered the same question as a child? *Why?*

I:8 Your Life Path Satisfaction Scale (self-quiz)
Rating: Rate your degree of agreement to the questions below (copy these into your personal *Life Path Maps Portfolio* and enter your ratings there), according to a 1 to 5 scale.

(1: Not at All; 2: Somewhat; 3: Neutral; 4: Usually; 5: Always)

1. I am confident in my ability to realize my dreams.
2. I have access to all the guidance I need in order to succeed.
3. I have a strong sense of my own life's purpose.
4. I am satisfied with major life decisions I have made.
5. I know where I want to be / what I want to be doing in the foreseeable future.

6. I generally set clear goals in my life and then strive to achieve them.
7. I have realized most of my life goals.
8. My dreams have been a valuable source of inspiration for me.
9. I have a clear sense of direction in my life now.
10. I know what my next step is and how to take it.

Add your scores for 1–10, then divide your total by 10. This is your Life Path Satisfaction Index Score as you begin your life-mapping process.

I:9 My *Daily Reflections and Dream Journal*
The first stage of a rites-of-passage adventure is known as the Separation stage. With chapters 1–3 *Tools*, you are taking "time out" to reflect about your Life Path in a way that "separates" you from your ordinary day-to-day routines.

Journal: Write your first Daily Reflections and Dream Journal entry, either within or separately from your *Life Path Maps Portfolio* pages.

What are you thinking and feeling as you enter into your life-mapping "time out"? What do you hope to learn about your life? What nightly dreams or key insights have you been having as you enter into this adventure in life mapping? If you are remembering some earlier dreams that could be relevant, record these, too. I encourage you to write in your Daily Reflections and Dream Journal pages regularly as you proceed through this book's *Tools*. Please note: It is helpful to record your dreams from the perspective of first person (I, me) and in the present tense (as if you are in the dream Now).

Chapter 2

LIFE IS . . . WHAT YOU MAKE IT: MAP YOUR LIFE PATH

We treasure the Hawaiian Islands as a tropical paradise. The lush landscapes, vital coral reefs, and rare biodiversity of this island chain have produced a cornucopia of beauty with a uniquely balanced ecosystem for millennia, making it one of the most desirable travel destinations in the world. Yet consider how this idyllic tropical paradise was birthed in a fiery forge. The Hawaiian archipelago offers an intriguing metaphor in how it was formed for how our own lives unfold. What we remember as the formative or island moments of our lives has for many of us included turbulent waters, sometimes teeming with volcanic undercurrents.

This chapter *Tools* guide you in mapping the formative Shaping Events of your life up to the present. This allows you to retrace the course you have forged that has established meaningful patterns and conditions still affecting you today. Instructions provided throughout this chapter for engaging with the *Tools* included at the end of the chapter will conduct you step-by-step through a series of basic techniques for composing your Life Themes Map. This mapping of your formative Shaping Events will uncover some interesting trends and Life Themes and it will establish a solid foundation for the rest of your life-mapping adventure.

This foundational chapter is more instructive in terms of primarily providing you with step-by-step directions than the other chapters of this book. This practical tutorial will guide you to compose your Life Themes Map, which is central for the rest of your self-discovery process with this book. So please forge on through the more standard procedures of this particular chapter so you can produce your unique Life Themes Map as a basis for further self-discovery.

Recalling and Mapping Your Shaping Events

Significant life events, or Shaping Events (SEs), are experiences from your life that, according to your own understanding, have shaped you into the person you have become. Reviewing your Origin Story (chapter 1, *Tool #1:6*) can help you to recover some of your Shaping Event experiences. Reflecting on your earliest memories can also help you to recall events and situations that have been influential to your growth and development.

The following factors are commonly identified kinds of Shaping Events. It may be helpful for you to review this list lightly, taking note of any significant, shaping sorts of memories it evokes for you.

- Formative influences (e.g., parents' values, educational experiences)
- Role models, both positive and negative (e.g., teachers, parents, friends, family members, coaches)
- Strong emotions (e.g., love, caring, fear)
- Challenges, traumatic events, or unforeseen tragedies (e.g., illness, painful experiences, loss)
- Trial and error, learning life lessons from your own or others' mistakes
- Faith, religion, or spirituality
- Romantic experiences (e.g., dating, marriage, divorce)
- Children
- Environmental influences (e.g., places, moves, travel)
- Life-changing beliefs and experiences (e.g., religious exploration, military service, Alcoholics Anonymous, philosophical studies, sports involvement)
- Major successes, rewards (e.g., graduation, new jobs, promotions)

I invite you to begin your Life Path mapping by composing a list of some of your key Shaping Event memories as they occur to you, using the space provided with Chapter 2, *Tool #II:1*. As you build your list, use the Age Line worksheet provided with *Tool #II:2* to plot the ages you were at for each of the events you have listed while you continue to reflect.

Using an Age Line (*Tool #II:2*), start mapping your Shaping Events by simply placing an *x* or a notch along this central line for every event you recall. The Age Line reads from left to right, indicating from birth to your present age chronologically. Place the age you were when an event occurred below each *x* or notch along the Age Line. You can also place a number above the same notch on the Age Line to keep a record of the order in which you recall your events. This way you can go back to add events after covering a certain time frame just by adding the number of the newly recalled event at the appropriate chronological Age Line position. Also keep a descriptive account for each event you are including on your Age Line. You can use the template given with *Tool #II:3*, using your event numbers from your Age Line along with a brief description of each event so you will be easily able to recall and recognize the event you are referring to during later steps. The section that follows includes instructions for you to make a complete log or record of these Shaping Events by using the template from *Tool #II:3*.

An easy way to start generating your list of Shaping Events is by thinking back to those early life experiences that "have shaped the person you have become." Then move forward and/or backward chronologically along the Age Line as you recall other significant Shaping Events or situations from your life.

Some people find it more natural to start in the middle years or even near to where you are at today in your life, marking a notch that represents a Shaping Event on the Age Line and then working forward and backward along your Age Line. However you begin with marking your events chronologically along the Age Line and keeping a descriptive account of your events in your Shaping Events

Record, feel free at any point to either add an event from an earlier period or to go back and fill in a specific time frame more fully. If you recall more than one Shaping Event that occurred in the same year, use decimal points to subdivide the year and/or number these same-year events with small letters as you record them chronologically within a year (e.g., *Ages* 21, 21.5, 21.75; or, *Event* 3a, 3b, 3c, etc.).

> Number and briefly label events in your List of Shaping Events (*Tool #II:1*) and in your Shaping Events Record (*Tool #II:3*) before continuing. Also begin mapping your Shaping Events along your Age Line, using the graph format given with *Tool #II:2*.

Remember, this is YOUR life-mapping process. Please take all the time you wish to recall and reconstruct a meaningful, fully "loaded" record of some of your most significant Shaping Events leading up to today. At the same time, bear in mind that it is not necessary nor is it even really possible to "get it all" onto your List of Shaping Events and your Age Line. There is no complete or more "correct" (or, incorrect) set of memories for you to map. At this stage, what matters is for you to include a sampling of the most memorable events that have influenced you in your life.

Some life mappers will find it natural to mark many events along their Age Line, while others will find it just as natural to recall only a few. Regardless of your age, people are different in this respect. Alex, for example, was a twenty-one-year-old who mapped over one hundred twenty events, while Marnie, over sixty years old, mapped only eight. There is no right or wrong way to do this, just your way! Also, people often ask whether the Life Map they construct today would be different from one they might have constructed at an earlier time or from what they would construct sometime later. Of course, whenever you compose your Life Maps with these procedures they will be unique, depending on the sorts of experiences you are focusing your attention upon in your life at the current time of your reflections. That is fine. What matters for purposes of life mapping overall is for you simply to reflect on your Shaping Events retrospectively, from your present point of view.

> Review the events you have recorded along your Age Line for *Tool #II:2*. Are there additional events that come to mind that you wish to include? Add these additional events to your List of Shaping Events (*Tool #II:1*) and to your Shaping Events Record (*Tool #II:3*), and map them onto your Age Line (*Tool #II:2*) before continuing.

Logging Events in Your Shaping Events Record

As you retrace your life's Shaping Events by marking the ages of these events or situations along your Age Line, it is valuable for you to include a basic description of each of these events for your future reference. *Tool #II:3* provides a format you can use to compose a full descriptive log of your Shaping Events.

To enter an event in your Shaping Events Record with *Tool #II:3*, simply transfer event numbers from your List of Shaping Events (*Tool #II:1*) that you have marked on your Age Line (*Tool #II:2*). For each event, write a brief, explanatory description. Answer the following question, about each event: *In what way(s) has this event or situation influenced or shaped the person I have become?*

Charting Positive and/or Negative Impacts of Your Shaping Events

Notice the blank, square boxes between the Age an event occurred and its description in my own personal sample of Shaping Events Record entries below. These boxes are there for you to record your "impact rating" for each of your Shaping Events, which I will describe next. *Tool #II:4* allows you to map not only when your Shaping Events have occurred but also your retrospective perception of the relative positive and/or negative impacts each of these events has had upon "the person you have become."

Age Line Sample:

SE#	1	2		3	4
Age	4	6		13	15

Shaping Events Record Sample (Use the format included with Chapter 3/#III:3):

SE#	Age	Rating	How this event was a turning point
#1	3		I fell off a booster chair and lost my four front teeth; it was significant because it made me feel self-conscious about my appearance from then forward, even to now, because my teeth did not grow back until I was nine.
#2	4		We lived less than a year in Sacramento. This was a critical time for me because I experienced creative freedom. I remember chasing a horse truck down the street on my tricycle with my piggy bank in one hand, expecting to buy a horse! It was a mixed bag, though: I remember my father severely punishing my sister because she didn't want to go to school her first day. She was six.
#3	13		My father was transferred (yet again!) so we moved to near Niagara Falls. This was a critical time for me at school because I tried to change my "nerd" image by dressing "cool" and trying to fit in with a more popular crowd.
#4	15		I was Assistant Director for a high school play. My English teacher/theater director Mr. S. inspired me to love literature, teaching, and theatre. I developed creative leadership skills. I also had excellent friends in the cast and crew.

Your Shaping Events Impact Chart is a visual graphic worksheet illustrated with *Tool #II:4*. Copy and create this worksheet grid in your own Portfolio journal or use the template provided in the *Life Path Maps Portfolio Toolkit*. This worksheet includes dashed grid lines numbered up and down along the left side of the chart, ranging from -5 to +5; use the Age Line itself to represent a zero (0) or a "neutral" impact rating on this Life Map.

To create your own basic Life Map of your Shaping Events using the chart shown with *Tool #II:4*, first simply transfer your events chronologically from your *Tool #II:2* Age Line, placing the number of each event from *Tools #II:1 and #II:2* onto the Age Line of the Shaping Events Impact Chart. Remember to also record your age at which each event occurred under the event's number on the Age Line of your Shaping Events Impact Chart for *Tool #II:4*.

Now then, for every Shaping Event you have listed and described in your Shaping Events Record (*Tool #II:3*), pause to reflect and then add, into the blank box following the age you have recorded for each event, your "impact rating" for that Shaping Event. Refer back to your description from your Shaping Events Record as you reflect on how, to you, this event has been influential in "shaping the person you have become." This process of providing an impact rating or score for your shaping events and then scaling their impacts from -5 to +5 on your Shaping Events Impact Chart (using the Life Map format from *Tool #II:4*) allows you to retrace the positive and/or negative impacts of these significant events from your life over time. This is a primary benefit of life mapping.

You can represent and record an event's impact rating on your Shaping Events Impact Chart simply by placing a pencil mark or an *x* vertically just above (+1 to +5 = positive) or just below (-1 to -5 = negative) or else right onto (0 = neutral) the Age Line corresponding with your age when the event or time frame occurred. This lets you scale the relative positive and/or negative weighting of the event as a shaping factor in your life from your present, retrospective viewpoint.

The following story about Dana, who was a foster child in a punitive foster family situation until she liberated herself when she was eighteen, illustrates the method as well as the value of retrospectively scaling the positive and/or negative impacts of your Shaping Events. Dana's case also illustrates how and why you might choose to rate a single event as both positive and negative at the same time.

Case Story: Dana

Dana was mistreated as a foster child until she freed herself from her foster home "prison" on her eighteenth birthday. The excerpt shown below from Dana's Shaping Events Impact Chart (*Tool #II:4*) shows how she mapped the relative influence of her early Shaping Events. Dana plotted events on her chart according to how old she was when they occurred, numbering her events along the Shaping Events Impact Chart's Age Line. Dana also logged a brief description for each event in her Shaping Events Record. In the blank boxes included on the Shaping Events Record for each event (*Tool #II:3*), Dana rated each of her Shaping Events, scoring their impacts from -5 to +5, according to the degree to which, in retrospect, she perceived the event had affected her life as a positive and/or as a negative influencing factor. Notice in Dana's Shaping Events Record sample shown below how she has scaled the relative positive and/or negative impacts of her Shaping Events in the rating boxes for each event.

SE#	1	2	3	[4]	5	6	
Age	3	4.5	[6		16]	18	(49)

Age Line: *CASE EXCERPT: DANA*

Shaping Events Record Samples (Dana):

SE#	Age	Rating	How this event was a turning point
#1	3	+5	My earliest memory: Dad tossing me up in the air, laughing, smiling.
#2	4.5	-5	Parents divorced; I dearly loved my father and hated my mother. Mother never was one to explain things clearly; she just told me I would never see him again. I am still bitter and upset after all these years.
#3	6	5	Mother decided she couldn't raise me so she took me to a foster home; she told me it was temporary (it wasn't). Still bitter about this.
#4	6–16	-5	Day-to-day unhappiness, beatings, fear, feeling imprisoned. We kids could never please the adults who handed out the work; stripped away any sense of self-esteem . . . a miserable time. I plotted trying to get away.
#5	16	+2/-5	Ran away. I snuck over to a neighbor's, bought a bus ticket from $3.00 a week allowance I had saved for years, went to my mother's, but she turned me in to police as a runaway; the foster parents dragged me back until eighteen.
#6	18	+3	Told foster parents I was leaving; went to live with Mother and new husband (better than nothing). Mother had remarried and her husband had a job in Singapore, so I moved there with them until twenty-one for my "big getaway."

Dana also mapped her Shaping Event impact rating scores into her Shaping Events Impact Chart as shown in the excerpt below.

For the event of running away from her foster home when she was sixteen (SE#5 on her chart), notice how Dana charted the impact of that one Shaping Event as both +2 as well as -5, placing event marks (*x*'s) vertically both above and below this event's number (SE#5) on her chart. This double rating was important for Dana to

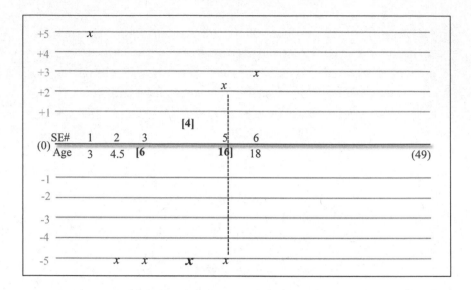

represent because it indicates how she felt this experience has influenced her life both positively (+2), due to the freedom she briefly felt, as well as extremely negatively (-5) because her mother turned her in and police returned her to the foster home "prison" for two more years. Notice how Dana also connected these simultaneous ratings on her chart with a dashed line crossing vertically through SE#5 on her Age Line.

I like to refer to the sort of Shaping Event that a life mapper rates as both positive and negative at the same time as a binary, *dynamic tensor event*. People often remember these more than usually heavy-impact binary Shaping Events as pivotal Turning Points that have marked major transitions in their lives. Dana's SE#5 tracks her attempt to escape her foster home at sixteen as a "dynamic tensor" Turning Point. In Dana's Shaping Events Record (*Tool #II:3*), she described the dynamically "tense" impact of that event: "I ran away to my mother's, but she called the police and the foster parents dragged me back until I was eighteen."

Chapter 3 *Tools* will guide you to identify your own Turning Points.

So far, Dana's example follows principles I have already presented. Notice in Dana's Shaping Events Impact Chart sample also, though, how Dana recorded her SE#4 as a *situational time frame* rather than just as a single event, spanning on the Age Line from ages six to sixteen. This was the time period between when Dana's mother sent her to the foster family until she initially tried to run away.

You can plot a situational time frame on your Shaping Events Impact Chart (*Tool #II:4*), if you wish, just as Dana did. Simply place square brackets along your Age Line to frame the age range involved, then number that time period by centering a reference number for the bracketed time range (also in square brackets) above the Age Line, as shown in the bold numbering for Dana's SE#4 in her chart.

Notice as well in the above example how Dana rated the situational time frame denoted by her SE#4 on her chart as -5 throughout by placing a bold, larger than usual *x* along the -5 impact line associated with her bracketed time frame of SE#4.

Case Story: Orene

Orene is a very spiritually motivated elderly woman who grew up in the Appalachian Smokey Mountains of West Virginia. When Orene was sixteen, she developed black lung disease and doctors told her she would have to move far away to the mountains of Colorado in order to improve her health. Orene married at sixteen and then moved to Colorado with her husband. When I asked Orene, when she was eighty-one, to rate the impact of her black lung diagnosis at such a young age and being sent away to survive, I expected her to answer, "-5." Instead, Orene's face lit up as she beamed, "+5!" Then she thought a little more and said she would actually rate the impact of that experience as both -5 as well as +5.

Orene explained:
Because if I hadn't gotten black lung disease, I would have never left West Virginia and come to Colorado, but that was the best move of my life! Sure it was difficult—there were plenty of hard times—but that illness happening when it did, it was a blessing in disguise!

Plotting impact ratings on your Shaping Events Impact chart provides you with a clear, visual tracking of some of the important Ups and Downs that have occurred in your life so far. The next phase of charting your Life Themes Map, with *Tool #II:5*, will make this life-mapping process for revealing trends and patterns that have occurred in your life experience even more meaningful for you.

Discovering Your Life Themes

Once you have recorded and charted retrospective impact ratings for your Shaping Events with *Tools #II:1–4*, you are ready to begin transforming your Shaping Events Impact Chart worksheet into your Life Themes Map. *Tool #II:5* asks you to review your Shaping Events Record and to sort your Shaping Events into personally meaningful *kinds* of events. As you group your Shaping Events into recurring types of life experiences that have been meaningful for you, create your own personally meaningful labels to describe each of these categories; these are your Life Themes.

Your Life Themes are those recurring kinds of life experiences or situations that have been highly influential in shaping you as the total, dynamic individual you are today. For example, if several of the events you have logged in your Shaping Events Record have involved school and, maybe later, college experiences, you might choose to name one of your Life Themes as *Education,* or perhaps *School*. It is important for you to assign your own personally meaningful names for these distinctive kinds of events in your life. Use whatever terms or phrases intuitively well describe these Life Themes for you within the context of your own life history.

Some commonly identified Life Themes include: *Family, Education*, *Religion* or *Spirituality*, *Relationships* or *Romance*, *Travel* or *Moves*, *Medical* or *Illness*, *Friends*, *Work* or *Career*, *Military*, and *Sports* or (for example) *Basketball*. This is neither a diagnostic nor an exhaustive list; again, feel free to name your Life Themes in whatever way feels personally relevant. Your Life Theme titles should ring true and make sense for you of the specific kinds of

Shaping Events you have identified with your List of Shaping Events as some of your common shaping factors. These Life Themes should encapsulate for you the typical kinds of life experiences you have listed in your Shaping Events Record.

A Life Theme label could name from just one to a grouping of several of your Shaping Events. Mercedes, for example, grouped several of her Shaping Events within a Life Theme she named *Life Lessons*. This helped Mercedes recognize a meaningful recurring pattern in her life. Mercedes realized that her *Life Lessons* events always followed difficult life ordeals and that they also usually preceded major moves.

Scott, whose Life Metaphor of *Hard Knocks* I shared in chapter 1, had been involved in only one romantic relationship, with a woman he married, but she divorced him within a year. Scott does not regard marriage or romance as a separate Life Theme at all; he names a *Family/Marriage* Life Theme that includes experiences involving his parents and siblings along with that one brief romantic relationship.

Some of you will name only a few Life Themes while others may identify quite a few, just as some people map only a few Shaping Events while others record many. It doesn't matter. There is no "right" way of approaching this process, only what feels right to you and helps you illuminate meaningful trends or recurring kinds of situations and events in your own Life Path. Elena, at age seventy-five, charted eight Shaping Events that she grouped into four Life Themes, while Alex, at twenty-three, charted over one hundred-twenty events that he sorted into nine Life Themes! The pattern that emerges from your own subjective mapping will be meaningful and illuminating to you, whatever its form. So please, name your Life Themes in whatever manner feels intuitively meaningful to you.

> Complete *Tool #II:5* before continuing.
> (Sort your Shaping Events into kinds of situations
> or events and name your own Life Themes.)

Color Coding Your Life Themes

At this stage you are ready to explore how mapping the flow of events comprising your Life Themes can reveal significant patterns in your life. Returning to your Shaping Events Impact Chart (*Tool #II:4*), you can now use colored pencils or markers to color code your already charted Shaping Event markers—these are the x's or the event points on your Shaping Events Impact Chart—according to your Life Themes.

Assign a distinctive color for each of your Life Themes and color over the *x*'s on your chart according to which Life Themes they represent. The template for *Tool #II:6*, which is your completed Life Themes Map, provides a key for you to fill in to assign different colors for each of your Life Themes.

The sample below illustrates this process using textured and gray-toned lines instead of colors for this print version, but please use colored pencils or markers for your own hand-drawn Map.

To represent on your Life Themes Map (*Tool #II:6*) how your Life Themes have patterned over time, simply use these same Theme colors to draw lines connecting your same-Theme event dots (your Theme-colored *x*'s). This lets you visually reveal how your thematic Shaping Events have been connected as Life Theme trends.

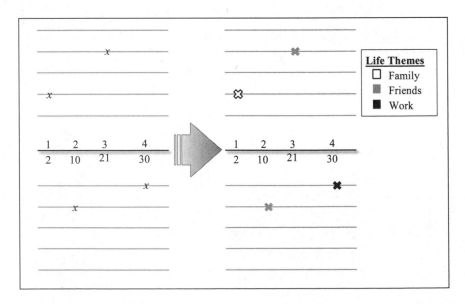

Connecting the Dots

The Life Theme-coded Shaping Events Impact Chart shown below with a boxed key connects same-Theme events from the above example. In this case, only SEs #2 and #3 are of the same Life Theme of *Friends*, gray-tone coded as indicated in the key. The format shown below represents these two, same-Theme event points as connected by a Theme-coded line. In this way, the connecting line indicates how the *Friends* Theme has "shifted" in its impact values over time, from including a -2 event at age ten to a +4 event at age twenty-one.

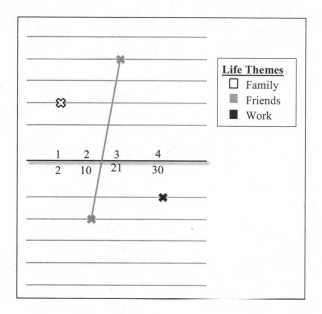

There are several factors to consider in "connecting the dots" of your Life Theme event points on your Life Themes-coded Shaping Events Impact Chart. Shaping Events of the same Life Theme that have occurred near to one another in terms of when they have occurred in your life or that are adjacent on your Shaping Events Impact Chart make sense, usually, to represent as a connected trend or thread. Do this by simply drawing a same-Theme colored line that connects these points on your chart.

Same-Theme events that are widely separated on a chart, however, especially when several events of different Life Themes have occurred between them, may not feel to you as if they are connected meaningfully to one another in your life history as a definite Life Theme trend. Rely upon your own intuition to guide you in considering when to represent a sequence of same-Theme events as a trend by drawing a color or texture-coded Life Theme line to connect them; or, rather, you may choose to leave them unconnected in order to represent that these events were separate and unrelated, where that feels more appropriate.

With chapter 3 *Tools* you will map further meaningful elements of your Life Path including your own Life Chapters. This will more fully reveal how your Life Themes have interwoven throughout your overall Life Story up to Now.

Add Image Icons to Personalize Your Life Themes Map

A fun way to personalize and creatively embellish your Life Themes Map (*Tool #II:6*) is to add or paste computer clip art images or magazine pictures, or your own artwork as you please, to symbolically represent your Life Themes with regard to their influences on "the person you have become." Simply insert or paste clip art icons or hand-drawn images onto your Life Themes Map, placing these above or below the Age Line where the Life Themes they represent are prominent in your Map. You can also include these icon images in your Life Themes key for easy reference. Please refer to Scott's Life Themes Map (on page 7) and Will's (on page 9) for examples of how to use these sorts of image icons to represent your Life Themes on your Life Themes Map.

If you would like to convert your hand-drawn Life Themes Map into a computer-generated Life Themes Map by using Excel or a comparable spreadsheet computer program (see instructions in the following section), you can then also insert clip art images, or paste them by hand if you prefer, onto your computer-generated version of your Life Themes Map where they are appropriate.

How to Create an Excel Chart to Represent Your Life Themes Map

All of the life-mapping charts illustrated in this book were initially composed by hand, by people who used markers or colored pencils such as I expect you have done so far as you have created your Life Themes Map. I have converted the hand-drawn charts into the computer-generated graphic charts shown in the book simply by entering information about the Shaping Event Impacts and Life Themes indicated in the hand-drawn charts onto an Excel spreadsheet that allows me to generate automatically color-coded Life Theme Maps using various Excel chart formats.

Excel is a Microsoft Word PC spreadsheet and chart-making software program. It is also available through Apple as an IPad download or as Apple Numbers. *Tool #II:7* provides step-by-step, illustrated instructions that guide you to create a spreadsheet with Microsoft Excel so that you can generate your own electronically color-coded Life Themes Map "line chart."

Still, you may prefer the freedom and the artistic license of hand drawing, so there is no need to generate a computer Excel chart. You might rather creatively embellish, expand, or modify your hand-written Life Themes Map in whatever form is most fun and meaningful to you.

> Complete *Tool #II:6* before continuing.
> (Compose your Life Themes Map based on your completed Shaping Events Impact Chart. Include color- or texture-coded Life Theme trends and add icon images to represent personally meaningful aspects of your Life Themes.)

Congratulations! You have created your Life Themes Map using the template shown with *Tool #II:6*. This is your base level Map that will serve as a solid foundation for the rest of your life-mapping journey; yet, there is much more for you to discover from here.

Much Ado about Something

Life is indeed what YOU make of it! I hope you are beginning to appreciate the value of life mapping; so far, you have discovered how thematic threads of your life experience have influenced the person you are today. It can be helpful to review the past so you may go forward with greater awareness and clarity into a future of your more conscious design.

Chapter 3 *Tools* will reveal to you the unique Life Story you have forged in your Life Path to Now. The rest of your life-mapping adventure with this book equips you to *Live Your Dream, Now!*

Chapter 2 *TOOLS*

Your Life Path Portfolio

II:1 My Shaping Events
Journal: Compile a list of your Shaping Events (SEs). These are the influential events or situations in your life that have meaningfully influenced the person you have become. Please note: Don't worry about recording *every* Shaping Event you have experienced. Representative examples of various *kinds* of significant experiences in your life will be sufficient to let you begin your life-mapping process.

At this stage, you do not need to concern yourself with recording your Shaping Events according to a timeline of which came earlier or later. If you prefer to list your Shaping Events in their order of occurrence in your life, that's fine, but you do not need to yet. For now, number the events (see the *Sample* below) according to your order of recalling them.

Simply provide below (continue on the following three pages, as needed) a list of meaningful events from your life that have "shaped you as the person you have become." You may move forward and backward through your life as you remember various influential situations or events. Several pages are provided so you can list as many or as few shaping events or situations as you choose (of course you can also add additional pages if you need to):

> *Sample: (#1/4yo): fell from a booster seat into the dining room table; lost 4 front teeth*
> *(#2/ after birth): incubator baby for 2 weeks; weighed 2.5lb*

II:2 Map Your Shaping Events along Your Age Line

Mapping: Create a timeline of your Shaping Events (SEs) by using the Age Line below to represent the ages you were at when each event you listed for *Tool #II:1* occurred. Simply place the NUMBER for each event you have listed in *#II:1* above the Age Line and write your AGE at the time when the event occurred just below its corresponding number along the bottom side of the Age Line.

SE#
_____

Age   ( )
(0)   ↗
                                                    Current
                                                      Age

II:3 My Shaping Events Record

Make a Record of the Shaping Events that you have listed and charted with *#II:1* and *#II:2*. Include your retrospective rating and a description of the relative impact of each event on shaping the person you have become.

Sample: #1/4yo +2/-3 *I fell from a seat booster and knocked out my top four front teeth (-3), but this led to a lot of positive attention that showed me how much my parents really cared (+2).*

SE#	Age	Impact Rating	Event description/Explanation of rating
—	—	—	_____
			_____

II:4 My Shaping Events Impact Chart

Mapping: Create the chart shown below in your Life Paths Mapping journal or use the template in your *Life Path Mapping Portfolio Toolkit* (chapter 2, *Tool #4*). Include five lines above and five lines below a central Age line. Use a pencil to mark dots or *x*'s on the grid according to your rating scores for the relative impact of each Shaping Event you have listed in your Shaping Events Record (*II.3*). Transfer the chronological information from your Age Line (*II.2*). Indicate your impact ratings on the grid lines above and/or below the Age Line for each numbered event as either positive (0 to +5), negative (0 to -5), or neutral (placing an *x* upon the Age Line as a 0 rating).

You may rate an event as duplex—having had both positive *and* negative impacts—by marking both ratings on the grid lines above AND below the Age Line, vertical to the age of the event on the Age Line. Use a ruler to vertically connect the positive and negative rating dots or *x*'s for duplex events.

+5 _____

+4 _____

+3 _____

+2 _____

+1 _____

SE# _____

Age   ( )

−1 _____

−2 _____

−3 _____

−4 _____

−5 _____

II:5 My Life Themes

Review your list of Shaping Events from chapter 2, *Tool #3*. Sort these events into KINDS of events by naming categories that are meaningful to you. Assign a descriptive name for each of these KINDS of events; these are your Life Themes. Create two columns in your Life Maps Portfolio journal or in your *Life Path Maps Portfolio Toolkit* for chapter 2, *Tool #II:5* as shown below. Write in your names for each of your Life Themes and then list the set of Shaping Event numbers from *Tool #II:3* that you would group within each Theme.

Sample: EDUCATION   *{#s 3, 5, 6, 9, 10, 11, 12, 24}*

    LIFE THEME   **SE#s from chapter 2, *Tool #3***

    _____   _____

    _____   _____

II:6 My Life Themes Map

Mapping: Transfer your information from *Tool #II:4*. This time, color code the marks you have made for your Shaping Events according to the Life Themes to which you relate them. You may also wish to connect same-Theme colored event markers with same-colored Theme lines to reveal trends that have occurred in your life in relation to your Life Themes.

    Assign colors to your Life Themes in the key.

+5 _____

+4 _____

+3 _____

+2 _____

+1 _____

SE# _____

Age   ( )

−1 _____

−2 _____

−3 _____

−4 _____

−5 _____

KEY: My Life Themes Color

☐ _____   ☐ _____   ☐ _____

☐ _____   ☐ _____   ☐ _____

☐ _____   ☐ _____   ☐ _____

II:7 Creating an Excel Chart to represent your Life Themes Map
Create an Excel data spreadsheet:

Step 1. On an empty Excel spreadsheet, type "Age" into column A (upper left corner) on the top row of cells. For columns B through as many columns as you need along the top row (#1 row), type the names you have created for each of your Life Theme categories. (See the *Sample Excel spreadsheet* excerpt shown below.)

Step 2. For each vertical column, input information in the appropriate cells. Type in ages when each of your Shaping Events occurred under column A. Type your impact rating scores (-5 to +5) for each Shaping Event within the appropriate Life Theme column. (For example, see that at *Age 1* in the *Sample Excel spreadsheet* below, an event rated with an impact score of +4 occurred associated with a *Family* Life Theme.)

Please Note: To plot binary or dynamically tense impact score ratings for a single event (e.g. +5/-5 for an event), *create two horizontal Age rows with the same Age value for the same event.* Insert the *positive* impact score (0 to +5) into one row under the related Theme of the event and insert the *negative* value (0 to -5) for the same event and Theme on the second line. (For example, see *Age 3* in the *Sample* below, where for an event that occurred at *Age 3*, the person rated this single event as both +2 and -3 under the *Family* Theme.)

Tip: To extend color-coded Life Theme lines on your Excel chart, insert additional, incremental Ages under column A, and repeat the same rating value for all of these Age increments under the same Theme. (For example, you could insert Ages 12, 12.5, 13, 13.5, and 14 all with +4 values under the *Family* column to generate a *Family* color-coded line spanning this Age range.)

Sample Excel spreadsheet:

	A	B	C	D	E
1	Age	Family	Career	Education	Spirituality
2	1	4			
3	3	2			
4	3	-3			
5	6			5	
6	10				4

Select Your Information and Create a Chart from your Excel spreadsheet:

Step 1. Click and drag with your mouse to highlight all of the information you have entered onto your spreadsheet including the Age column (A) and all of your Life Theme columns (B to *n*). Start at the upper left corner of the spreadsheet including the AGE header cell and drag down and across to include all Theme columns and rows (but do not include the Excel row-numbering column that precedes (A). Or, you can also start from the bottom right corner from as far as your chart includes information and drag upwards and to the left to include the AGE column heading and the names for all of your Life Theme columns. Be sure that the Age heading cell appears in white as not selected to properly format the Age Line. (Only certain chart formats including Scatter Line and Stacked Area formats will plot your information using the Age line as an *x*-axis.)

Step 2. With your information selected as above, Click: *INSERT*, then Click: *Chart* from the top menu. Select: *Scatter Line Chart*. (You could alternately or also click on *Stacked Area Chart* to experiment with another format for representing your life map information). Your chart will appear in a small box within your spreadsheet. It will automatically be color coded according to your Life Themes, showing the unfolding of your events along an Age Line.

Step 3. To create a separate page for your chart, Click: *Move Chart*; then Click: *New Sheet*.

Step 4. Click within your Excel chart to select any item you wish to further format or embellish. Insert or adjust text boxes to write in Life Chapter titles or other text; you can also change colors of the Life Theme lines, change your lines to add thickness or textures, modify your key and its event markers, insert clip art images, or format the background to provide a background color to your Life Map.

Tip: To format the scale dimensions of your Chart:

> **Y axis:** set Maximum = 5, Minimum= -5, Major unit = 1;
> **X axis:** Min = 0, Max = (your current age), major unit = 5, minor unit = 1

Chapter 3

LIFE IS . . . AN EPIC JOURNEY: DISCOVER YOUR LIFE STORY AS A MYTHIC QUEST

Myth is the stuff our lives are made of, for myths are made up from the stuff of our lives. Our life experiences are never truly empty or devoid of meaning, as meaning is the very substance of human consciousness. Humans "make sense" of every experience and any sensation; that is at the core of our cognitive, bio-cultural adaptation. We are symbol makers; we interpret our way through every moment to which we apply our thoughts or language.

> Complete *Tool #III:1* before continuing.
> (Try experiencing five minutes without using language.)

Life is filled—I should say, riddled—with meaning and shot through with purpose, regardless of your philosophy. Now then, perhaps the most fundamental human experience to which we attribute meaning is our own Life Story. From our cumulative life experiences, we construct a cohesive whole—a personal narrative that is greater than the sum of its parts. This Life Story that you constantly build, modify, and add significance to is given structure by the interpretive frameworks you apply to it, including Life Metaphors and Life Course Schemas.

The meaning and structure you assign to your Life Story runs deeper—though—than partial metaphoric images and skeletal outlines.

We live out our lives in mythic proportions; we are heroic protagonists set upon a universal Quest.

With chapter 2 *Tools* you have embarked upon your Life Path mapping adventure. Already you have discovered how your personal journey has a thematic texture to it. Your recurring Life Themes show definite patterns as they interweave through meaningful life transitions. You have reflected on the relative impacts of formative events that have shaped you as the person you are today. Some of your Life Themes and shaping experiences have presented you with difficult obstacles and challenges; others have brought to you much joy, upliftment, and change.

This chapter's *Tools* will conduct you further through your life-mapping odyssey. You are ready to reveal the dramatic unfolding of your Life Chapters up to Now and the dynamic, mythic plotline active within your own Life Story.

You are about to discover how the life you are living has parallels with some of the greatest stories ever told. First, then, allow me to help you identify and name your personally meaningful Life Chapters.

Your Life Chapters

Refer to the list of Shaping Events you have included in your Shaping Events Record (*Tool #II:3*). Now ask yourself, which of these events or situations were of such a critical magnitude in your life that you feel you were "not the same person" before and after these events occurred? These are your Critical Life Events (CLEs), or your Turning Points.

> Complete *Tool #III:2* before continuing.
> (Identify your major Turning Points.)

Turning Points are those pivotal moments or situations that bring about major transitions in our lives. Because these events have been so monumental, consider the quality of life experience that has transpired *between* your major Turning Points to be your Life Chapters. From birth to your first Turning Point, for example, might have been a relatively calm time in your life (though, of course, not for everyone), compared to the next phase that followed. Perhaps you would name the first chapter leading up to this first Turning Point then as *Innocence*, or more simply as *Childhood*, while you might title your second chapter as *Challenges* or *Lessons to Learn*. These are common sorts of first and second chapter titles people use. Still though, it is important to this self-discovery process for you to provide your own titles to each of your Life Chapters; ask yourself what a most meaningful title would be that best encapsulates your personal experience during each of these time frames between your major Turning Points.

Now then, to develop your Life Themes Map from chapter 2 into your Life Story Map with this chapter's *Tools*, begin by simply drawing vertical dotted lines on your Life Themes Map passing through the age points on the chart for each age at which your Turning Points have occurred. In this way, you will identify these Turning Points on your Life Themes Map (chapter 2, *Tool #6*) as "chapter boundary" markers.

Next, as the author of your own Life Story script, I encourage you to compose meaningful titles that encapsulate the nature of your life experience occurring BETWEEN each of the Turning Points you have marked (e.g., between birth and your first Turning Point, then between that first Turning Point and your next Turning Point, etc.). From here on, think of these named time frames as your own significant, personal Life Chapters.

Complete *Tools #III:3–5* before continuing. (Mark and compose Life Chapter titles on your Life Themes Map. Add these to your Life Themes Map (page 43) if you wish, or transfer a photocopy of your Life Themes Map to a separate Life Story Map, including titles for your Life Chapters.)

Your Life Story

Where are you currently positioned within your Life's unfolding legacy? Are you standing "at the Threshold" of new adventures, feeling ready and waiting to embark? Are you ambling forth as usual from day to day, engaging one situation and the next without a clear destination or plan? Are you charging forward daily, actively living your Dream? Or, are you caught within a fiery pit, feeling stuck and forlorn or facing shadowy Dragons?

Life mapping uncovers the narrative script of your Life Story to Now. There are three conventional story genres that people almost always unconsciously draw upon in composing Life Chapter titles for their Life Story: Epic Adventure—either Comic or Tragic—and Episodic. Your sequence of Life Chapter titles most likely represents one of these three basic storylines.

If your Life Chapter titles trace your passage from facing and overcoming challenging obstacles so you have eventually achieved positive outcomes, your Life Story as you reconstruct it to now has been an Epic-Comic Adventure. If your Life Chapter titles are situational, without a unifying dramatic plot except for decades or moves or relatively random "marker" events, you have cast your Life Story as Episodic or "picaresque." If your chapter titles reflect a period of deep descent and major hardships from which you feel you have not yet fully emerged, you may construe your Story from your current perspective as an Epic-Tragic Adventure.

The archetypal psychologist James Hillman recognized these same three genres—he called them comic, picaresque, and tragic—in his psychotherapy clients' case stories. In *Healing Fiction* (Spring Publications, 1998), Hillman explains how the same person may have more than one of these genres active in their life at the same time:

> . . . even while one part of me knows the soul goes to death in tragedy, another is living a picaresque fantasy, and a third is engaged in the heroic comedy of improvement.

A Dweller at the Threshold

Where are you at within your ever-unfolding Life Story right Now? I have found that most life mappers regard themselves as having achieved a state of relative balance or of having resolved most of their earlier challenges from the present vantage point from which they reflect back on their lives. No matter how challenging or turbulent their life situations may have been, the majority of life mappers—not everyone, of course—reconstruct their Life Story up to the immediate Present either as an Epic-Comic Adventure or as an Episodic Adventure that has brought them to at least a temporary plateau of resolution, relative balance, or higher awareness within their current Life Chapter.

This awareness that you have achieved a state of relative balance from the point of view of your retrospective current outlook is known as "dwelling at the Threshold." This is a positive result from achieving a holistic overview of your life by reflecting on your life experience as a connected story up to Now. This is why it can be so helpful to reconstruct and map your Life Story in the first place. When you look back at how you have successfully met difficult challenges in your life up to Now, you are better able to frame your life experience within a greater perspective as a unified whole, with a cohesive and purposeful Story.

Sara, for example, is the young woman I mentioned in chapter 1 who engaged with life mapping in a university class. She told me near the end of the class that at first she had not wanted to participate in any form of life review because of traumatic abuse in her childhood. After completing her Life Story Map, Sara says she began to feel "much more optimistic" about her future compared to her challenging childhood. Sara realized how she had already overcome many challenging hardships in her life so that she has become stronger than she had realized.

A Tragic Story

Remember Scott's story of *Hard Knocks* from chapter 1? Scott mapped his Life Story as an Epic-Tragic Adventure. His sequence of Life Chapter titles reads as follows:

> *Prelude /Expectations/ Holding Onto Expectations/ Over the Rainbow/ No Pot of Gold.*

Notice Scott's reference to "Over the Rainbow" from *The Wizard of Oz*. Like Dorothy, Scott took a bold leap to another world when he moved from his family's home in Colorado to California, trying to "jump start" his work life after a disappointing series of layoffs. But he soon lost the California job, too, so he returned home—potentially like Dorothy, too, except that Scott felt tragically defeated: *No Pot of Gold*. At the time of his life-mapping reflections, Scott portrayed himself as a tragic antihero trapped in a fatalistic Life Story.

Comic Adventure Tales

Most people's sequence of Life Chapter titles reconstruct a dramatic storyline like Scott's, except they usually express an Epic-Comic story with a happy ending. Below are several people's Life Chapter sequences that illustrate this usual trend. Notice how earlier chapter titles lead dramatically to resolution chapters (shown in bold) at the time of the person's life-mapping reflection.

MARNIE *Childhood (0–6), Hell (6–23), Lessons (23–42),*
     Giving Back *(42–Now/58)*

HAJ *Innocent Childhood (0–6), Preparation (6–18),*
     Awakening *(18–Now/22)*

MINDY *Paying Off Heavy Karma (0–9), Slowly Waking Up (9–38),*
     A More Awakened Consciousness *(38–Now/45)*

LOGAN *Oblivious (0–3), Growing Up (3–18), Desperate (18–38),*
     More Desperation (38–46), **Happy** *(46–Now/58)*

LILITH   *Well Loved/Happy (0–2), Loss (2–21), Breaking Free
(21–23), The Hell Years (23–25), Searching for Security
and Change (25–27), Struggle and Growth (27–30),
Learning to be a Mom (30–35), Looking for Love
(35–37), Recovery (37–43), Looking for Independence
(43–46),* **Finding Self Again** *(46–Now/52)*

The sequences of Life Chapter titles shown above illustrate how most people—more than 90 percent of the over five hundred cases I have recorded to date—reconstruct their Life Story, as an Epic-Comic Adventure.

Episodic Adventures

Some people script their Life Story neither as Tragic nor Comic but rather as an Episodic or picaresque adventure. An Episodic storyline is less driven by purpose, at least on the surface; it is punctuated by apparently unrelated marker events such as by moves or by incremental time frames.

People who hold a Cyclic Life Course Schema might title their Life Chapters according to regular, recurring phases such as by decades or by seven-year cycles. This is one version of an Episodic framework. Persons oriented to a Seamless Life Course Schema mind-set might at first resist or choose not to assign Life Chapter titles at all, preferring to identify their Turning Points just as episodic page-turners, key moments of transition to which they have responded as needed.

The protagonist in an Episodic story—like Don Quixote, for example—could appear to be set upon a winding road with relatively unconnected adventures. Unforeseen and often surprising, unplanned events punctuate the Life Path of the Episodic character. The Episodic storyline, however, like an Epic Adventure, does have an underlying direction; it has a story to tell, even if the purpose or plot development may not be so obvious on the surface.

The following Life Chapter sequences are from actual life mappers; they illustrate the Episodic Life Story genre:

SHEILA	*Downfall (5–7 yrs old)—The Calm (8–15)—The Rolling of the Wave (15–Now/22)*
SAMUEL	*1st Decade (0–10)—2nd Decade (11–20)—3rd Decade (21–Now/23)*
MARJORIE	*Childhood (0–11)—Teenage Years (12–18)—Young Adult (19–21)—Adult (22–Now/33)*

So everyone does it, but why? What is the value of reconstructing your Life Story in the form of a conventional narrative genre? This human penchant for framing our life experiences in terms of Life Themes, Life Chapters, and stock narrative forms places our stories onto a broader canvas and illuminates our sense of adventure and purpose. It may also highlight individually some of your most important life lessons.

I hope you have discovered by now how your Shaping Events have not actually been occurring helter-skelter. They are patterned according to your very reconstruction of them in memory. They have come to "mean something," at least to you, in relation to your recurring Life Themes and with respect to your own values, your goals, and your basic outlook on life. Happy or sad, "going somewhere" or feeling "stuck at a proverbial crossroads," your story—dramatically reconstructed by the sequence of Life Chapters you have mapped—reveals who you are as a character. Your Life Story tells of where you are at today and how you have come to be where you are. You are the key protagonist within your Life Story, poised at the Threshold of future adventures within your Epic, Episodic, or Tragic (to Now) Quest.

When you reflect on your Life Story—framing it as a genre, embellishing its themes and plot, gleaning its direction and potentials—you deepen your understanding about your life as a whole; you recognize its inherent value and honor its significance.

You are staking a claim: this is My Story. Having done so, you are free to mine the resources brought nearer to the surface of awareness by your life-mapping self-discovery process. We are miners as life mappers, digging, panning for the gold deposits embedded in the rich loam or fluid streambeds of memory.

Complete *Tools #III:6 & 7* before continuing. (Reflect on how your Life Story has unfolded as an Epic-Comic, or Epic-Tragic, or as an Episodic Adventure.)

Your Parallel-Mythic Life Story

Now that you have mapped your Life Story, you have developed a more conscious awareness of yourself as a dramatic character. Who are you in your Life Story, really? You are an Epic or Episodic life adventurer, a heroic (or sometimes tragic) protagonist with a meaningful tale to tell. Your adventure, your road through life, is neither fully haphazard nor isolated. It is thematically scripted and infused with meaning; it is mythic.

Like Dorothy of Kansas or Harry Potter of the Hogwarts School of Witchcraft and Wizardry, finding yourself—and in the process mastering inherent powers that benefit yourself and others—you go forth. Or like the picaresque Don Quixote tilting at windmills, chivalrous though sometimes misguided, you go forth. Or even as a tragic figure who has fallen into Descent and not yet resurfaced but who is learning vital lessons from within the depths of your despair, you go forth.

Myth is transformational; rendering your Life Story as myth prepares you to better realize your potentials.

Now then, the next life-mapping *Tool* I invite you to engage with is a Parallel Myth technique (*Tools #III:8–12*). This *Tool* guides you to discover the dynamic potentials of your Life Story as a Mythic Quest. You will arrive at a Personal Myth Narrative Statement (*Tool #III:11*) by composing a synopsis of your Life Story based on a popular storyline with which you can identify. This Parallel Myth comparison reveals more distinctly how you have forged your life as a protagonist of epic proportions.

Your Life Story is a unique inflection of themes and pathways intrinsic to the very nature of humanity and the cosmos! As a meaningful story, your mythic adventure contributes to the entire history of humanity; it cannot do otherwise.

> Complete *Tools #III:8–12* before continuing. (Engage with the Parallel Myth technique.)

The following story illustrates the value of highlighting the mythic qualities of your Life Story.

J. D.'s Epic-Comic Life Story: "Something Special"

J. D. was a twenty-four-year-old African American who undertook life mapping to consider his options while contemplating his future after college. J. D. reconstructed his Life Story according to sixteen Shaping Events. He identified eight Life Themes and named three Life Chapters: *Growing/Molding (ages 4–14)*, *Rough Times (14–18)*, and *Enlightenment (18–24)*. Ever since his parents' divorce when he was four, J. D.'s biological father was absent from his life. J. D. was exposed to an uncle's and other neighborhood gang activity from a young age in a rough inner-city neighborhood in Chicago. Positive influences during his early "Molding" years were few but included a supportive grandmother, playing basketball with hopes of a professional career, and—foremost—caring for his younger brother, whom J. D. cherishes as his closest friend and has always felt responsible toward.

J. D. identified his parents' divorce as the first of three critical Turning Points. He rated their divorce as simultaneously -5 and +5: negative, he says, "because I always wanted to have my father in my life," yet positive because "since then, I'm determined to be there for my kids." This early vow, manifested in J. D.'s close, protective bond with his younger brother, motivated many of J. D.'s later choices.

Between his parents' divorce and his next Turning Point—that is, through his Molding/Growing years in Chicago—J. D. and his younger brother survived several harrowing incidents involving neighborhood crime. Twice while J. D. was in his early teens people drew guns against him and his brother: once during a robbery of their home, and less than a year later one day while he and his brother were outside playing in their backyard. The second gunman threatened to kill them both to retaliate against a relative of J. D.'s who the gunman claimed had raped his sister. Fortunately, both times the situation was defused; J. D. rated the robbery event as -4, explaining: "I wouldn't be here today if I had found the pistol I went looking for to protect my brother."

When J. D. was fourteen, his mother moved to Colorado with a new husband, bringing J. D.'s younger brother with her. At fifteen, J. D. joined them, mainly to protect his brother from his stepfather's abusive behavior. That move was a second Turning Point in J. D.'s life. "It changed everything," he says.

J. D.'s second Life Chapter, *Rough Times*, was a mixed bag for him and his brother. He enjoyed a wider, less racially segregated community in Colorado and he continued to play basketball, which brought him self-discipline and the opportunity to attend college. After being kicked out of his mother's house for fighting with her about the abusive stepfather, J. D. moved in with an uncle who dealt drugs and further exposed J. D. to criminal activity and a "bad crowd." To support himself and his brother during that time, J. D. says, he turned to dealing drugs himself. After his younger brother's success with basketball in high school, though, J. D. moved back in and lived more peaceably at his mother's, so he could be "a better role model" for his younger brother.

J. D. described his third Turning Point as an epiphany connected with a traumatic car accident near the end of his senior year of high school. One day a "crackhead" uncle who had joined the family from Chicago asked J. D. to go with him to score drugs. J. D. let his uncle drive his own car while he rode in the passenger seat. The uncle ran a stop sign and totaled J. D.'s car. J. D. rated this terrible accident as "+5." Here was his reasoning:

Because a lot of things happened around that. I became more spiritual because my younger brother had been spared; and

I would have been sitting in the back seat if we had seen my brother and taken him with us. Also, it led to getting a new car for college, so I looked at the situation as a message to my uncle that he needed to change his ways (even though he didn't).

J. D's moment of epiphany was followed by the Life Chapter that he titled *Enlightenment*. J. D. attended a community college before transferring to the four-year college his younger brother was attending after gaining all-star ranking playing basketball. At his new school J. D. met a girlfriend and others who exposed him to several future career opportunities. Also during this chapter, his mother attempted suicide. J. D. rated that event as positive as well as negative: "because if she had died our kids would not have grand-parents on our side."

J. D.'s girlfriend became pregnant but miscarried after she and J. D. dissolved their affair. J. D.'s younger brother chose not to finish college when he married and moved out of Colorado. His younger brother's move was the final Shaping Event that J. D. mapped. He concluded his mapping reflections with the comment: "We're both now doing our grown man thing."

J. D.'s Parallel Myth mapping, shown below, brings the mythic elements of his Life Story into clear focus:

"Something Special"

1. Molding/Growing	2. Rough Times	3. Enlightenment
Where he got a lot of ideas about discipline and family structure, and he became involved in sports.	Lowest of all lows; Doing things he never thought he'd have to do just to get by. Times of conflict, but they drew him and his brother even closer.	About growth and being open-minded, about learning and taking life for what it is. Don't take things for granted, enjoy life, and moving forward to the future. Everything he's gone through in the past has led to this point.

J. D. chose the popular science fiction story *The Matrix* as his Parallel Myth. Reflecting about some parallels between *The Matrix* plot and his own Life Story, J. D.'s Personal Myth Narrative Statement (see *Tool #III:10*) portrays himself as the heroic protagonist of his Epic-Comic Adventure:

> The hero, once freed, became more open-minded and saw things as they were. He was able to move forward and help others. He went through rough times, having to choose between saving his girlfriend Trinity and helping the world. He did what he believed, not what he was told to do. He followed his heart.

J. D.'s choice of *The Matrix* as a parallel story for his life makes sense of the title J. D. assigned to his Life Story overall: "Something Special." Like the heroic Neo from *The Matrix*, J. D. has attempted to bring his family from dark, chaotic beginnings into a New Reality of caring and prosperity.

Several years after J. D.'s life-mapping reflections, he contacted me one day via email. J. D. has become a successful life insurance salesperson living with his wife, daughter, and son in Florida. He told me his life-mapping "time-out" had helped him define and later to realize his goals. He liked being able to help others as an insurance agent to plan for their own futures and to achieve well-being for their families.

Your Mythic Quest

Now then, are you ready to discover how you are never really alone on your magnificent Life Story Quest? Chapters 4 and 5 will invite you to meet and greet your very own ensemble cast of mythic Archetype characters who will accompany you as "parts of Self" you have developed in the normal course of enacting specific social roles related to your situational Life Themes throughout your life.

I invite you to proceed from this point forward with full awareness that you are the central heroic protagonist within your own

Life Story. Step forward to claim and then to fulfill your mythic Quest, to accomplish your deepest sense of Purpose and Mission in this lifetime.

Chapter 3 TOOLS

Your Life Path Portfolio

III:1 My experience of five minutes without using language
Journal: To gain insight about the subtle role and influence of LANGUAGE in your everyday, moment-by-moment life experience, I invite you to practice spending five full minutes (or more, but five is a lot for this!) WITHOUT USING LANGUAGE, at all. That means no talking, no decoding someone else's speech either to you or to another, no reading of signs, no "thinking in language" or talking in your head. Can you do it? To the extent that you can, what do you experience? Journal about your insights from this practice.

III:2 My Turning Points
Review your list of Shaping Events from *Tool #II:1*. Which of these events were so "critical" in your life that you feel you were not quite the same person before and after this event or situation occurred. These are your Turning Points. Identify them according to the number and rating information you assigned in your SE-Record and describe their impact in your Portfolio Journal or in your Toolkit for *Tool #III:2*, using the format illustrated below.

SE#   Age   Rating   How this event was a Turning Point

—— —— —— ————————————————

—— —— —— ————————————————

III:3 Marking Turning Points on My Life Themes Map
Mapping: Photocopy your Life Themes Map from *Tool #II:6*. Paste this copy of your Life Themes Map (enlarged, if you wish) onto a blank page in your Portfolio Journal or in the space provided with your *Portfolio Toolkit* for *Tool #III:3*. Using a ruler and pencil or

by inserting dashed vertical lines if you are using Excel computer software, place a dashed vertical line from the top to the bottom of your Life Themes Map at every age point at which one of your Turning Points occurred. This adds Turning Point markers to your Life Themes Map.

III:4 Naming My Life Chapters

Journal: Reflect on the time frames that have occurred in your life BETWEEN the Turning Point events you have marked for *Tool #III:3*. Name a Chapter Title for each of these time frames, as if you were the author of a story about your life; for remember, you are!

III:5 My Life Story Map with Life Chapters

Mapping: Using your Life Themes Map with your Turning Points marked vertically from *Tool #III:3*, write in your Life Chapter titles (or insert text if you are using Excel) along the top of your Life Story Map, between your Turning Point lines.

III:6 My Life Story Genre

Journal: Has your Life Story to Now been unfolding more as an Epic-Comic Adventure, as an Epic-Tragic Adventure, or as Episodic?

III:7 My Life Story as a Conventional Adventure Story

Journal: Describe how your Life Story has unfolded as an Epic-Comic, an Epic-Tragic, or an Episodic Adventure (or, as whatever combination of these seems relevant to you).

III:8 My Parallel Myth Map, Step 1

Draw vertical lines as needed to represent your Life Chapter dividers and then write in brief chapter descriptions, using third person ("he" or "she") to describe what each of your Life Chapters has been "about," on a Parallel Myth Map as illustrated below in your Portfolio Journal or in your *Portfolio Toolkit* for *Tool #III:8*.

Chapter Title I	Chapter Title II	Chapter Title III	Chapter Title IV
(3rd person description of events) . . .			
Name of Parallel Story:			
Narrative Statement (merging the parallel story with your Life Story)			

III:9 My Parallel Myth, Step 2: My Personal Parallel Myth

Read through your sequence of Life Chapter descriptions several times from Step 1 above (*Tool #III:8*). Consider the sequence of your chapter synopses to be a story script, and ask yourself: *What popular storyline (e.g., a from fictional novel, a historical biography, a classical myth, or a movie plot) does my story remind me of?* Write the name of this Parallel Myth story in the space under your chapter synopses included on your Parallel Myth Map from *Tool #III:8*, as illustrated above.

III:10 My Parallel Myth, Step 3: My Personal Myth Narrative Statement

Merge or "collapse" your Life Chapter synopses descriptions from *Tool #III:8* with the storyline of the Parallel Myth you have identified with *Tool #III:9*. Using a heroic name to refer to yourself as the heroic protagonist of your own Life Story, write a brief OVERVIEW description of your Life Story to Now that incorporates relevant elements from the parallel story you have named. Place your Personal Myth Narrative Statement into your Parallel Myth mapping chart from *Tools#III:8 and 9*.

III:11 My Parallel Myth, Step 4: My Life Story Title

Compose a Title for your Life Story as you have described it in your Parallel Myth Narrative Statement from *Tool #III:10*. Write your Life Story Title at the top of your Life Themes Map (from *Tool #II:6*).

III:12 My Mythic Life Quest

Journal: After taking some time to reflect deeply about your Parallel Myth Narrative Statement from *Tool #III:10*, boldly declare your own Mythic Life Quest as the heroic protagonist of your unique Life Story in your Portfolio Journal or in your *Portfolio Toolkit* for *Tool #III:12*.

Chapter 4

LIFE IS . . . AN ENSEMBLE CAST OF MYTHIC CHARACTERS: MEET YOUR ARCHEMES

It has always appeared self-evident to me that after the ending of the movie version of *The Wizard of Oz,* Toto is going to be okay. The movie does not explicitly arrive at this conclusion. Mrs. Gulch, the mean neighbor, will still be next door after Dorothy recovers from the tornado blast, and even though Dorothy has matured in her appreciation of "home," Toto has still invaded the neighbor's garden, and the sheriff's papers calling for poor Toto's surrender have already been served.

So, why after the conclusion of this Epic-Comic Adventure do we understand that Toto will survive? I propose it is because the *Wizard of Oz* is not really about the separate life experiences of Dorothy, Toto, the Scarecrow, the Tin Man, and the Cowardly Lion; nor is it about their real-life counterparts including Auntie Em, the carnival magician, and the three affable farmhands. It is about the dynamic constellation of these archetypal character figures and their human counterparts, acting together as an ensemble cast.

Toto will no longer be taken away because the total dynamic of Dorothy's ensemble cast has shifted ground as a key outcome of her mythic adventure. As the central heroic protagonist Self, Dorothy has successfully identified, strengthened, and recombined several of her own unconscious "persona Archetype" qualities that were previously underdeveloped and scattered, not to the tornadic winds exactly, but into unintegrated character shards. In Carl G. Jung's terms, *The Wizard of Oz* is a tale of Dorothy's individuation through the maturation and integration of her own unconscious, archetypal parts of Self within what I will call her Total Self System.

Dorothy initially lacks the courage she needs to confront her irate and spiteful neighbor. She lacks the heart to forgive both her neighbor and her aunt and uncle for not standing up to the sheriff about Toto, and she lacks the wisdom to stand her ground responsibly—at "home" in the power of her Self. Dorothy also lacks the maturity to acknowledge that she needs to better control her pet's behavior.

> Dorothy: *Run, Toto, run!*
> Witch of the West: *. . . He got away!*

I love the scene just after Toto escapes from the Wicked Witch of the West's forbidding castle. It is Toto who gathers the three subliminal figures of Dorothy's psyche, who are actually images from her inner archetypal cast projected into Ally character roles.

In the process of rescuing Dorothy, each Archetype Ally exercises precisely those qualities needed to strengthen and mature themselves as elements of Dorothy's Total Self System. The Scarecrow "has an idea" for how to rescue Dorothy. Tin Man cries about Dorothy's imprisonment, motivating the team to act by expressing his deep love. The Cowardly Lion, though still with some degree of trepidation as he needs encouragement from the other two, marches forth to lead the group snarling, wagging his tail assertively. All the while Dorothy's diminutive but powerful *animus* companion Toto recombines the three and herds this integrated constellation of Dorothy's inherent strengths to confront the negative, shadowy agency of the Wicked Witch. They face the menacing Negative Force together, with the combined force of their integrated oneness of purpose. How could they fail?

> All (Together): *The Wicked Witch is dead!*

The triumph is complete. Back in the Wizard's palace in Emerald City, the Wizard awards each member of the heroic ensemble with a totemic symbol to reinforce his or her individual Archetype Strengths. Ultimately a Higher Power—via the Magi Guide Glinda, Good Witch of the North—helps Dorothy realize she "has had the power all along." All she has needed was to harness the combined Strengths of her integrated, individuated Total Self, symbolically grounded in those precious ruby slippers.

Dorothy returns to conscious awareness in Kansas, her Epic-Comic hero cycle fully accomplished. Dorothy has left her now harmoniously Self-integrated Ally qualities in control at Oz, within the field of her personal unconscious domain and available for her to call upon as needed. She brings back with her to the "conscious = Kansas" realm—we have Jean Houston to thank for this observation in *The Wizard of Us* (Atria: 2012)—her companion *animus* Toto along with a more mature, potent new vitality of Self that will not be easily thwarted.

Your Ensemble Cast of Mythic Archetype Characters

Who are the heroic cast of characters you yourself may befriend as you have set forth upon your Life Story Quest? Allow me with this chapter's self-discovery *Tools* to introduce them to you; or rather, allow me to assist you in reacquainting your Self with your very own internal cast of primary Archetype Allies.

Within your Life Themes Map and your Life Story Map that you have composed via chapter 2 and 3 *Tools*, you have already revealed your inner archetypal parts-of-Self; though you have yet to recognize and name them as such. You need next only to identify them and to contemplate their roles in your life as ensemble cast members of your Total Self System.

> Complete *Tool #IV:1* before continuing.
> (Describe personal qualities you can associate with each of your Life Themes.)

"The Twelve" Universal Persona Archetypes

Carl G. Jung describes Archetypes as:

> . . . primordial types, that is, universal images that have
> existed since the remotest times. (The Collected Works of
> C. G. Jung, Vol. 9/1, Bollingen Series 20, Princeton University
> Press, 1969.)

Archetypes are universal energy modes or ideal-forms that
exist in both of what Jung called the collective and the personal
unconscious. Within our psyche, these figures manifest as personified images of animals, persons, or objects; they can also appear
as abstract symbols representing latent quality potentials. A man's
anima Archetype, according to Jung, and a woman's *animus*, for
example, are opposite sex mental images that could appear in your
dreams or as traits you project onto others, expressing "inner feminine" traits of a man or unconscious masculine traits of a woman.
Shadow Archetype figures may show up in your dreams as dark, usually same-sex animals or as people who manifest personality traits
that you have difficulty "owning" in yourself or that you unconsciously suppress.

In "The Concept of the Collective Unconscious," delivered to
the Analytical Psychology Club of New York City in 1936, Jung
explained:

> There are as many archetypes as there are typical situations
> in life. . . . When a situation occurs which corresponds to a
> given archetype, that archetype becomes activated.

Now then, we can bring this subject of Archetypes into perspective with regard to your life-mapping process. This chapter's *Tools*
invite you to explore how the Life Themes you have identified in your
Life Themes Map (*Tool #II:6*) are recurring kinds of situations that,
when prominent in your life, activate unconscious ROLE IDEN-
TITY qualities that are facets of your overall personality makeup.

You have developed your own role "personas" in large part from observing others in similar role-types throughout your life. Think of your role personas as situational modes of self-expression that coexist as parts-of-Self within your own internal ensemble cast of characters, each of them associated with one or more of your primary Life Themes. These situational and role-based, archetypal character modes are primary ensemble cast members for you, just as the Tin Man, Scarecrow, and Cowardly Lion reside in Dorothy's repertoire of situational Archetype Allies.

Below is a table of twelve universal Archetype character figures recognized by the former Avalon Archetype Institute of Boulder, Colorado, as adapted by one of its faculty, Debra J. Breazzano, MA, LPC. This chapter's *Tools* invite you to associate some of the members of this universal unconscious pantheon with roles you typically enact and outlooks you might express in connection with your recurring situational Life Themes.

Twelve Universal Persona Archetypes

The Avalon Archetype Institute system of persona Archetypes, named as adapted by Debra J. Breazzano, MA, LPC

	Creation	Maintenance	Dissolving
Earth	Elder Leader	Artist	Healer
Air	Lover	Idealist	Communicator
Fire	Warrior	Golden Child	Teacher
Water	Nourisher	Descender	Mystic

Can you intuitively recognize these twelve Archetype characters from the table above as being potentially active within your own Total Self System? They each could manifest as either masculine or feminine images and they could express themselves energetically in either Strength (positive) or Shadow (inhibited or negative) modes. Everybody has access to all twelve of these orientations; they exist as potentials within the cognitive architecture of human consciousness. The social roles you have developed in relation to your recurring

Life Themes affect which of these outlooks will be prevalent or more expressive of You in a particular situation.

As a cultural anthropologist, I surmise that this inner pantheon of role-typed persona Archetype forms is a product of human social and cognitive evolution. This set of Archetypes represents necessary status and role types in any society. Any society requires parents, leaders, warriors, artists, innovators, mystics, healers, communicators, and the rest of these twelve primary role identity forms. They have therefore developed as cognitive types within the collective history of human cultural and social development.

Dr. Charles Bebeau, founder with his wife Nin Bebeau of the Avalon Archetype Institute, derived this pantheon of twelve primordial Archetypes directly from ancient Sumerian mythology and astrology (Bebeau & Bebeau, Archetypes of Soul [Soul Matrix], Vol. 2, CreateSpace, 2015). Charles Bebeau established that these twelve psychological Archetypes comprise a system of primary, universal persona Archetype forms operating in what Jung called the universal, collective unconscious.

The specific arrangement of Archetype persona figures depicted in the table above reflects their "elemental" nature. They represent— horizontally, from left to right—the three phases of any energetic process: Coming into Being/Creation, Maintaining, and Resolution/ Dissolving; along with—vertically, from top to bottom—the four elemental qualities of Earth, Air, Fire, and Water. Jung recognized this same intersection of "trinary" and "quaternary" Archetype energy modes. As such, the Twelve Universal Archetype figures referred to in the table above represent a comprehensive, dynamic system of character images that exist at least in latent or potential form within everybody. They may present and express themselves situationally within your conscious behavior and attitudes as well as in your unconscious or subconscious levels of awareness.

Individual expressions of these twelve role-based character Archetypes can appear according to a wide range of personally meaningful forms that you might experience or name idiosyncratically. For example, an Orphan Archetype could represent for someone a GOLDEN CHILD figure. You might perceive your inner IDEALIST as a Jester or perhaps as a Pilot or Astronaut, since this Archetype is associated with pushing beyond boundaries and with air or flight. Tin Man as Dorothy first encounters him in *The Wizard of Oz* represents a Shadow LOVER image, while the Cowardly Lion represents a Shadow WARRIOR and Scarecrow appears to be a Shadow TEACHER form.

I invite you to imagine all of the Twelve Universal Archetypes as character figure "elements" included within your personal Alchemist's toolkit. The personality qualities you associate with these elementary potentials housed within your psyche are available for you to befriend. You can "alchemically" activate, combine, and integrate their potentials to help you advance further in the direction of your goals. This and the next chapters' *Tools* equip you to consciously initiate this sort of metaphorically alchemical process.

Debra J. Breazzano's "The Twelve Universal Archetypes," included as the appendix at the end of this book, provides detailed descriptions for each of the Twelve universal persona Archetypes. The table presented later in this chapter (pgs. 74–75), also by Debra J. Breazzano, provides a concise overview of the Twelve archetypal persona figures' most characteristic traits.

Tool #IV:2 invites you to associate each of the Life Themes you have included in your Life Themes Map (*Tool #II:6*) with one or more of the Twelve Universal Archetypes described in the table below and in the appendix, based on your free association with some of your own personal qualities that are relevant to your Life Themes.

If one of your Life Themes is *Parenthood*, for example, you might associate that Theme in your life with qualities of the ELDER LEADER Archetype. Perhaps you will intuitively associate a *Romance* or *Relationship* Theme with the LOVER Archetype, either in Strength/positive or in Shadow mode. Note that the DESCENDER is an Archetype that has both Strength and Shadow qualities of its own. Many people associate the DESCENDER Archetype with Life Themes associated with challenging situations or with hardship-oriented perspectives.

Meet Your Archemes

There is a natural association between your Life Themes and the Twelve Universal Archetypes that derives from the day-to-day roles you enact and the perspectives you have (arche-)typically adopted within your recurring sorts of life situations.

For example, if you were to train to become a doctor or a nurse for your career, you might naturally draw upon universal—and your culture's specific versions of—HEALER attitudes, behaviors, and ways of presenting yourself in this role. You would be likely to adopt some of these archetypal traits by observing other Healers and imitating—or sometimes by avoiding—their behaviors and attitudes, and from literature or movies that illustrate various portrayals of the HEALER Archetype.

You might associate an Archetype with one of your Life Themes based upon its Strengths (Mission or Qualities traits described in the table above) or because of its Shadow traits. ELDER LEADER, for instance, might resonate for you in relation to a Life Theme involving a parent figure, or family in general, or in relation to some authority figure or role model, either positive or negative in his or her impact, who has been a significant influence in your life.

For another example, you might associate a Life Theme of *Romance* with a LOVER Archetype. Alternately, your *Romance* Theme could instead resonate for you with Strengths (e.g., see Mission traits in the table below) or with Shadow traits of NOURISHER, DESCENDER, or IDEALIST, depending on your experience. You could also identify one or more of your Life Themes with some unique combination or "constellation" of the Twelve Archetype figures.

Please keep in mind as you associate these universal Archetypes with your Life Themes that each of the Twelve is a "superclass" sort of Archetype that might manifest for you as a more specific, idiosynchratic image. A Soldier Archetype image (in connection with a *Military* Theme, for instance) could resonate more directly as a personal Archetype for you than WARRIOR, while a Fireman or Wonder Woman might better depict a WARRIOR Archetype form for someone else.

Once you have associated each of your Life Themes with one or more of the Twelve Universal Archetypes (*Tool #IV:2*), from this point forward refer to the Archetype modes you have identified with your Life Themes as your primary, dominant Archemes (*Archeme* = Archetype + Life Theme). These personified, thematic role figures are members of your very own ensemble cast of Archetype characters! Your Archemes comprise your mythic cast of situational role Allies much like Dorothy's Tin Man, Scarecrow, Cowardly Lion, and Toto.

The more you can personify and learn to interact subconsciously with your unique Archeme parts of Self, the better you will be able to integrate them within your Total Self System. This integration can bring to you a greater sense of balance and harmony within your entire range of conscious and unconscious motivations and outlooks.

Complete *Tool #IV:2* before continuing. (Associate each of your Life Themes with one or more of the Twelve Universal Archetypes based on the table below and/or based on more detailed trait descriptions from the appendix located at the end of this book.)

The Twelve Universal Archetypes

		Mission	Shadow	Qualities
Earth	Elder Leader	Provides structure, leadership, authority	Judgmental, strict, critical	Linear thinking, status quo-based
	Artist	To beautify the world, giving form to spirit	Stubborn, passive-aggressive	Earthy, creatively inspired
	Healer	Healing spiritually or physically	Can be codependent caregiver	Sensitive, delicate, ritualistic
Air	Lover	To create transcendent partnership	Conflicted over relationship	Commitment to relationship
	Idealist	Help humanity, attain freedom	Rigid about ideals if denied	Visionary, far-reaching mind, intuitive
	Communicator	To link, be messenger	Chatterbox or silent treatment	Synthesizing, curious
Fire	Warrior	To pioneer, change	Aggressive or tactless	Fiery, assertive; loves challenge
	Golden Child	Heartful, charismatic, inspirational ruler	Needy, spoiled, arrogant	Draws loyalty, generous, dependable
	Teacher	Impart awareness, learn lessons	Perpetual student, argumentative	Expansive mind, traveler to learn

Water	Nourisher	Nurture of family, community, self	Selfish or martyrdom	Like Ocean, full, nurturing
	Descender	Embracing hardship, leading to growth	Controlling, fearful, depressed, stuck	Deep, intense, private, secretive
	Mystic	Redemption, revelation, wisdom	Addiction and boundary issues	Metaphysical, dreamy, empathetic

As a personal example of how it can be helpful to personify and engage with your Archemes, I have identified and consciously engaged with a DESCENDER Archeme persona within myself that I call "Little Linda." She is a member of my Total Self System who has occupied a shadowy region of my psyche, appearing to me in active imagination sessions as a young girl not ever wanting to become an adult. After I had engaged with her through an active imagination dialogue as a vital member of my Total Self, she spoke out consciously one day while I was attending a spiritual retreat. She introduced herself spontaneously—with my awareness and agreement—to one of my friends there, exclaiming, "Hi! I'm Little Linda, and I want to be a part of this, too!" My friend was surprised, but he immediately understood this was an honest sharing from an often-submerged part of my Self; so, he was pleased to welcome and to include her.

Mapping Your Archemes

The remaining *Tools* in this chapter guide you to compose and to reflect upon your own Archeme Map. You can add to your Life Story Map (*Tool #III:5*) by inserting Archeme names from the Universal Archetype table above, where your associated Life Themes have been prominent. Write your Archeme names onto your Life Story Map, either above or below the neutral Age Line depending on their relatively positive/Strength or negative/Shadow influences. Your resulting Archeme Map represents when your situational Archeme personas have been most active or influential throughout your Life Story.

You may recognize that some of your Archeme cast of characters may have helped you to advance and enjoy your life experiences; while others may have stunted your progress or held you back from realizing your goals or aspirations.

Archeme "voices" or their unconscious nudges can sometimes overlap or contradict one another. The *Devil on one shoulder and Angel on the other* metaphor is an apt depiction of this all-too-common condition of the archetypal human conscience. Especially where you have rated an event on your Life Themes Map as both positive and negative in its impact—as a binary, dynamic tensor event—this could indicate opposing or even polar-opposite Archeme influences pertaining to that Shaping Event.

For example, a person who has lost their job might rate that *Work* event's impact on their life as simultaneously -5 and +5, because while it may have impacted their income negatively, at the same time they may feel it freed them to learn new skills or to seek a new, fresh opportunity for growth and advancement. This person might associate the two Archetypes of DESCENDER and IDE-ALIST with the negative (-5) and positive (+5) "poles," respectively, of this same *Work*-related event of losing their job. Much like the proverbial Angel versus Devil scenario, having DESCENDER and IDEALIST as conflicting Archeme energies could result in the person having mixed feelings about this dynamically tense situation.

For another example from my own life, two of my Life Themes are *Education* and *Romance*. I associate *Education* primarily with a TEACHER Archeme. TEACHER qualities have played a positive, progress-oriented role through most of my life, present in every one of my Life Chapters from an early age as a "lifting" factor. *Romance*, alas, I associate alternately with positive traits of LOVER but also with DESCENDER and Shadow-IDEALIST Archemes. This constellation of complex or mixed Archeme influences shows up in my Archeme Map as a midlife series of emotional peaks (Ups) and troughs (Downs) that trace a sharply vacillating *Romance* thread.

For me, then, my TEACHER persona has been a valuable source of inner support I can turn to when the doldrums, or a Descent experience of emotional loss or separation, could otherwise pull me Down. I tend to shift into the "Teacher" mode—as my family and friends have aptly observed—when I face an emotional letdown. The dynamic tension created by the coexistence of these distinct Archeme parts-of-Self strikes a personally meaningful chord within my overall sense of identity or construction of Self. I recognize this internal dynamic conflict as "just part of who I am."

Life mappers frequently associate a DESCENDER Archetype with Life Themes that include usually negative impact events or with the negative poles of their binary events, especially with events they rate +5/-5. A DESCENDER Archeme could exert a negative influence that inhibits you from achieving certain desired outcomes, such as a stable romantic relationship or a satisfying work environment.

However, keep in mind that those same negative-seeming Archeme attitudes or character traits that most inhibit or impede your progress can also contribute vitally to your process of adaptation and development. They provide access for you to essential Life Lessons with regard to personal challenges that could help you to unfold remarkable strengths with transformational growth. Deleterious Shadow impulses and traits can truly hurt you only when you deny or try to hide them from your Self, or when you do not pay attention to or listen to them.

> Complete *Tool #IV:3* before continuing. (Which of your Archemes feel mainly positive or are associated with situations you have mapped above the neutral Age Line in your Life Story Map? Which feel mainly negative or occur as Shadow/ negative aspects of binary—e.g., +5/-5—events?)

Two Stories: Mindy and Thomas

Life Chapters are often distinct from one another by the range and combination of Archeme influences that are prominent within them. Within each chapter of your Life Story up to Now, the activation of specific situational Archemes either may have been helpful, or hindered your happiness or your capacity to accomplish your goals. Allow me to illustrate the value of Archeme Mapping for two individuals who benefitted significantly from completing their life-mapping journeys: Mindy and Thomas.

Mindy

Mindy was forty-two when she engaged in an intensive, nine-month life-mapping process. She described a Life Course Schema with four phases: Birth—Maturity—Death—Reincarnation. Mindy's Life Metaphor of *Life is Like a Racetrack Going Round and Round* along with her belief in reincarnation clearly expresses a Cyclic orientation. Mindy scripted her Life Story as an Epic-Comic Adventure with three Life Chapters: *Paying Off Heavy Karma* (ages 0–10), *Unconscious—Slowly Waking Up* (ages 10–38), and *A More Awakened Consciousness* (ages 38–42). She mapped twenty Shaping Events, grouped within five Life Themes: *Spiritual, Physical, Relationship, Education*, and *Relationship with Self*. Mindy associated these Life Themes with Archemes as follows:

Life Theme	Archemes
Spiritual	WARRIOR
Physical	DESCENDER
Relationships	NOURISHER, GOLDEN CHILD, and COMMUNICATOR
Relationship with Self	IDEALIST vs. DESCENDER
Education	ELDER LEADER, COMMUNICATOR, TEACHER, and MYSTIC

In Mindy's Archeme Map below, notice how Mindy associates members of her Archeme cast with positive and/or negative impact trends of her Life Themes. Mindy has placed Archeme names onto her Life Story Map according to the impact ratings she associates with these Archemes' related Life Themes. DESCENDER, for example, is an Archeme Mindy associates with several Life Themes that have consistently negative (0 to -5) impact values. Mindy places the label of DESCENDER, then, below the neutral Age Line and in an area on her Archeme Map that corresponds with the negative trends of these Themes.

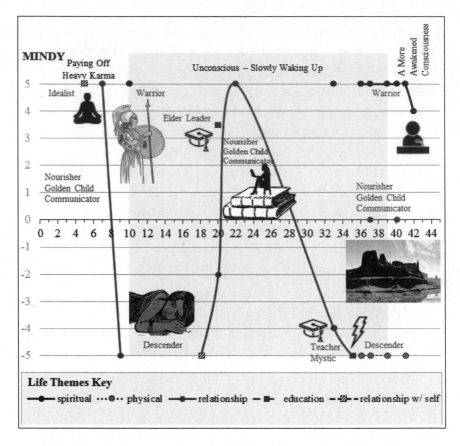

Mindy's Archeme Map revealed to her some interesting patterns. She mapped several Life Themes that include extreme-impact (+5, -5, or +5/-5) events. Mindy associated *Spiritual* events with a WARRIOR Archeme, with *Shaping* Events she always rated (+5). On the other hand, Mindy almost always rated *Physical* events as extremely negative (-5), and she associates her *Physical* Theme with a DESCENDER Archeme.

Notice how Mindy's *Relationship with Self* Theme shows a binary, dynamic tensor (+5/-5) pattern. Mindy associated IDEALIST with the +5 pole of her binary *Relationship with Self* events. She associated DESCENDER with the -5 impacts of these same events.

Mindy's Archemes of WARRIOR and DESCENDER appear from her mapping to be locked in a mortal conflict. Mindy journaled about how she often "feels torn" between these powerfully contrasting energies in her consciousness. She associates this duality with a persistent internal conflict she often feels between following her inner "spiritual nudges" versus being pulled down by the hard realities of day-to-day living. This inner conflict had led Mindy to make many rather sudden changes of direction in her relationships, in her physical locations, and in her jobs.

Mindy's education has been impacted by this inner conflict. She entered college intending to complete one major, believing this major to be a spiritual calling, but when she felt that her older sister who had graduated with the same major did not approve, Mindy quit college altogether, questioning college as a true spiritual calling.

Through Archetype Dialogue journaling, to which I will introduce you in the next chapter, Mindy came to understand how the internal conflict between her WARRIOR and DESCENDER parts-of-Self motivations related primarily to her dynamically tense Life Theme of *My Relationship with Self*. She realized that this conflict traced back to "mixed messages" from her early family life that had led her to develop this unconscious inner conflict.

Using a seven-step Archetype Dialogue Practice (see *Tools* included with chapters 5–8), Mindy used active imagination and journaling to explore the conflicting motivations of her WARRIOR and DESCENDER impulses. She found that both of these Archemes have sought to help her manifest "Freedom"; although, they have disagreed strongly as to what Freedom is.

To Mindy's WARRIOR Archeme, Freedom means to follow her spiritual nudges, regardless of social norms or risk. To her DESCENDER persona, quite by contrast, Freedom means not to feel bound by any potentially limiting condition or commitment.

Through Archetype Dialogue journaling, Mindy was able to connect with and to forge a conscious agreement between her WARRIOR and DESCENDER parts-of-Self. In her journaling, these two otherwise polarized Archeme energies agreed to work together to help Mindy to define and fulfill a shared Life Dream.

Since completing her life-mapping process, Mindy has in fact taken great strides; she has realized her Life Dream of becoming a public speaker on a national platform. Initially, she traveled around the country speaking on a wide range of health topics, all of which she deeply values. More recently, she has settled down to one relationship and to writing about and promoting various health topics online.

Mindy has become better able to make choices that provide her with a physical grounding while at the same time she remains attuned with her spiritual values and goals. She has realized it does not have to be one way or the other.

> Complete *Tool #IV:4* before continuing. (Do you recognize multiple or opposing-binary Archemes associated with one or more of your Life Themes?)

Thomas

At twenty-six years old, Thomas was in an intense period of preparing for graduate school when he embarked on his life-mapping

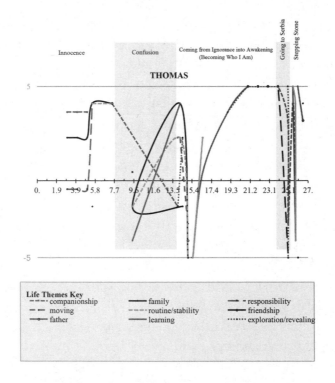

adventure. Thomas's Life Story Map shown on the previous page maps five Life Chapters interwoven by nine Life Themes. Each of Thomas's Life Chapters reveals a distinctive pattern in terms of the specific Life Themes active within the chapter and their patterns of relative positive and/or negative impact values.

Thomas's Life Chapter titles dramatically reflect these patterns: *Innocence* (ages 0–9), *Confusion* (ages 9–14), *Coming from Ignorance into Awakening* (ages 14–24), *Going to Serbia* (ages 24–25), *and Stepping Stone* (ages 25–26).

Thomas's Epic-Comic Life Story opens with positively valued Life Themes of *Companionship* and *Family* along with a slightly negative (-1 events) Life Theme of *Responsibility,* from ages three to five. In these early years, Thomas was given the responsibility to care for his older, mentally disabled brother. Thomas titles his first chapter *Innocence*, a period which took a dive into a much more complex second chapter propelled by his parents' divorce when Thomas was eight.

Thomas names his second Life Chapter *Confusion*. He maps for this chapter a sequence of dynamically tense swings. *Family, Learning,* and *Companionship* Themes all vacillate up and down as well as cross over each other with tumultuous, (+5/-5) valued, binary Shaping Events. Thomas's *Confusion* chapter culminates with the emergence of a new Life Theme, which he names *Exploration/ Revealing*. This Theme, of itself, is also binary; Thomas rates most of its Shaping Events as (+5/-5). *Exploration/ Revealing* events, for Thomas, have included stressful times that have nonetheless resulted in profound learning whereby, Thomas says, he has learned to "reveal myself to myself."

Thomas's father was hospitalized for a borderline personality disorder during much of Thomas's *Confusion* chapter (ages 9–14). A new stepfather introduced him to stimulating intellectual interests. But Thomas says he felt emotionally and intellectually "split" throughout this chapter. When Thomas was fourteen, his mother, brother, and stepfather moved out of state, leaving him alone with his father and a new stepmother just before his father was again hospitalized for a prolonged period.

Thomas calls his third Life Chapter, *Coming from Ignorance into Awakening: Becoming Who I Am.* This chapter opens with negative-impact Shaping Events for Thomas's Life Themes of *Family, Moving, Health/Craziness,* and *Father.* In this chapter, Thomas experienced a long period of intense personal growth and development from ages fourteen to twenty-four. He graduated from high school and then worked for the Forest Service on a fire crew for a few years, and after that he entered college.

Thomas was the first from his family to attend college, and this choice brought about an enormous uplift in his Life Story. This is evident with the *Learning* Theme that dominates Thomas's chapters 3 through 5 along with newly emerging Themes of *Routine/Stability* and, eventually, *Romance.*

Thomas enjoyed an extremely positive phase for nearly five years in college during which he met two best friends, a man and a woman. Thomas traveled internationally with these friends over college vacations, expanding his horizons. He developed a romantic relationship with his female best friend and they have since married.

At twenty-five, Thomas received a research scholarship to study abroad in Serbia for seven months. Thomas titles his fourth Life Chapter simply, *Going to Serbia.* He records a distinctive pattern in this chapter, which he calls a "blip" in his overall Life Story. While in Serbia conducting research about the use of language dialects there, Thomas experienced intense highs and lows that had the dramatic effect of "revealing" to Thomas aspects of his personality at once frightening and exhilarating, depressing and joyful. After nearly five years of having enjoyed close companionship and stability with his friends, he felt isolated and alone in Serbia. This helped Thomas appreciate how deeply he missed the sense of stability he had enjoyed with his friends in college.

Thomas's return from Serbia initiated the Life Chapter he was immersed in during the "time out," as he called it, of his life-mapping self-exploration. He called this fifth chapter, *Stepping Stone.* This chapter was about confronting his father and coming to terms with deep uncertainties he was feeling as he planned to marry and then to relocate for an out-of-state graduate program. During this chapter, Thomas confronted and resolved a deep, long-term question about his own mental health in relation to his father's condition.

"You're not me," his father told him point-blank, during a conversation Thomas initiated. Thomas said the sense of resolution this finally brought to him granted him the freedom to move forward.

Descent and upliftment: a dialectical, alchemical sort of struggle to forge beauty out of apparent ugliness, gold out of lead, well describes the Life Story of this intense young man who referred to himself as Thomas based on a mixed reference to both the enlightened Catholic scholar Thomas Aquinas and the disciple "Doubting Thomas."

Thomas's Personal Myth Narrative Statement from his Parallel Myth mapping compares his Life Story to that of the Buddha. It expresses the sense of accomplishment Thomas arrived at through his life-mapping reflections:

> Now the Hero has returned to his world and feels a strength,
> courage, and vision behind his method for living. He feels as
> if he were emerging from a deep water.

Descent with self-confrontation resulting in profound learning has been a direct outcome for Thomas, relating to several of his Life Themes.

Near the end of Thomas's life-mapping sessions, he expressed how he had been able to benefit from his life-mapping reflections and journaling by resolving his deeply buried fear that he might be susceptible to developing his father's mental illness. After achieving this "awakening," Thomas remarked triumphantly during his final life-mapping session:

> I feel compelled to step into the world, no longer afraid, or,
> at least not so afraid.

Thomas successfully Crossed the Threshold with his life-mapping odyssey, in mythic as well as in quite practical terms. As an outcome of his profound life-mapping reflections, Thomas felt ready to close one set of chapters and embark upon a whole new dimension of his Life Path.

Thomas has since completed two master's degrees (in Philosophy and in Anthropology) and a PhD in Anthropology. He is currently a professor and he continues to be a world traveler conducting international research studies along with his wife. Thomas is manifesting daily his Life Dream of lifelong learning; he has become as well a positive role model to others as a conscientious Teacher.

> Complete *Tool #IV:5* before continuing. (What patterns do you observe with respect to the Life Themes within Life Chapters of your Life Story and/or in your Archeme Map?)

Guardians of the Threshold

Joseph Campbell made a comment worth reminding you of at this fertile, Threshold-crossing passageway within your own life-mapping journey. As you set forth, aligned with your ensemble Archeme cast to more consciously conduct your Life Path as a mythic-heroic adventurer, please do be mindful:

> The adventure is always and everywhere a passage beyond the veil of the known into the unknown; the powers that watch at the boundary are dangerous; to deal with them is risky; yet for anyone with competence and courage the danger fades. (Joseph Campbell, *The Hero with 1000 Faces*, 1949)

Mindy's and Thomas's Life Stories and their Archeme Maps portray each of them as Epic-Comic adventurers poised at positive, defining moments in their lives at the time of their life-mapping reflections. In composing their Life Story Maps to Now, as you have done by completing the chapter 3 *Tools*, they achieved the vantage point of being Dwellers at the Threshold, prepared to go forth in life with greater strength, equipped with the insights and awareness their life-review process illuminated.

Like you, Mindy and Thomas discovered how recurring Life Themes have interwoven through meaningful, distinctive Life Chapters of their unique Life Stories. They were able to associate their Thematic kinds of Shaping Events with generally unconscious parts-of-Self Archeme traits.

Mindy and Thomas discovered how some of their Life Themes that they associate with specific Archemes have propelled them forward and tend to lift them "upward" in their lives at critical junctures. Other Life Theme situations and Archeme outlooks have triggered times of Descent or have exhibited Shadow Archeme impulses, magnifying their fears, disappointments, or frustrations.

After attaining their Dweller at the Threshold vantage point through their life-mapping reflections, Mindy and Thomas proceeded further. They learned how to consciously connect with and integrate their Archeme character Strengths and to benefit from the Life Lessons they had gained from reviewing their past, so they could proclaim and go forth to realize their Life Dreams. Drawing upon the combined Strengths of their Archeme Allies, both Mindy and Thomas crossed beyond the "Present-time," retrospective viewpoint Threshold they had achieved. They proceeded from there to reset their Life Paths toward achieving their highest potentials. They are successfully *Living Their Dreams, Now*!

You are now equipped to advance to the next stage of your journey: to Cross the Threshold you have arrived at from retracing your Life Story to Now.

There is a distinct danger to alert you to, though, at this pregnant Threshold-Dwelling juncture. To stop here or to remain fixed at or satisfied with your current Threshold vantage point, lingering too long at this "plateau," could lead you to Refuse your Call to proceed further, across and beyond the Threshold boundary.

The biggest part of your life-mapping rites-of-passage odyssey, as you aim to fulfill your Life Mission and Quest, is yet to come.

Before you can *Live Your Dream, Now!* you must yet "slay"—but I prefer to say, tame—your "Dragons."

Mythic allegories suggest that when anyone approaches to enter a field of higher consciousness, they can expect to encounter Threshold Guardians. That means you can expect to encounter both internal and external resistance to stepping forward beyond the plateau you have achieved. I can relate to this personally from a lucid dream I experienced around the time I embarked upon my own dedicated journey to write this book.

In my dream, I arrived at what felt to me like a "high-altitude" dimension of sublime beauty. I was in a misty, pale blue-violet-gold region where the air itself felt "rarified." I knew that a herd or a select group of amazing, Winged Horses inhabited this exquisite field of Higher Power. These were not just any Winged Horses; I knew intuitively that they served the Higher Powers directly to convey spiritual Masters or Guides on their errands as Coworkers with the Divine. That is why they were privileged to inhabit this pure region of the Heavens. With this awareness, I desired ardently to enter into the region of these Horses of Heaven, to be amongst them or to sit astride one of these fantastic Beings. Yet even as I formed this thought and approached the outer borders of their High Domain, suddenly Gremlins appeared!

With wide, pointed ears and flat, rodent-like faces and with small, bulging, black piercing eyes, these little Gremlins protected the boundary surrounding the rarified domain of the heavenly Winged Horses. I sensed intuitively that my heart and my motivation must be totally pure, or else I would be denied entrance and expelled by these Gremlins who then popped up everywhere I looked along the border.

I stepped back and kneeled down just to watch then, content not to advance any further.

I must have passed some inner test by not resisting or reacting with fear, defensiveness, or disrespect of the threshold-guardian Gremlins, for the next thing that happened was that two amazing, white Winged Horses approached from behind and to the right of where I knelt. One kneeled down gracefully on her front legs, to allow me to climb upon and ride on her bare back as she stepped gracefully across the boundary into the Horses of Heaven's domain.

It was a brief privilege, as after that I immediately awoke from the dream, my heart and soul overflowing with elation and gratitude.

I awoke from this inner witnessing of the powerful, raw beauty of Higher Consciousness and from encountering and being granted passage beyond the Threshold Guardians, with deep feelings of awe and humility. I realized then that if only I could accomplish my own life's purpose—whatever that might be in its entirety—well enough and with a pure heart, I might at some time later again be honored to visit this region of the "Horses of Heaven" and beyond.

One message I took away from my mystical Horses of Heaven dream encounter was that a deeper, higher phase of my life's journey had begun. So has yours, as you are now—at this vital juncture of your own life-mapping odyssey—a Threshold Dweller. Having completed Stage I of your life-mapping rites-of-passage cycle—which has been your initial Separation stage of reviewing your Life Story to the Present—I invite you to consider how you might purify your consciousness so you may approach your own Threshold Guardians, when they appear, with a proper intention.

Then, proceed!

Chapters 5 through 7 with their related *Tools* comprise Stage II, the Transformation phase of your life-mapping rites-of-passage adventure. This next, central part of your life-mapping adventure will conduct you through a Descent and Re-Emergence process of further self-discovery.

The *Tools* for this next stage of your journey will allow you to explore how you have experienced past transitions and will invite you to meet and engage directly with the dynamic energies of your ensemble cast of Archemes so you can enlist and enjoin them as Allies.

You have yet to confront—and when you approach them properly, to slay or tame—your Dragons.

This is a dangerous passage you are about to embark upon, slippery, requiring a Descent, so do be prepared! At the other side of this next phase of your self-discovery adventure, re-emergence and the potential to fully *Live Your Dream, Now!* will be clearly within your grasp, but it cannot be taken for granted.

Complete *Tools #IV:6–8* before continuing. (What are your own Threshold Guardians? What significant dreams have you experienced prior to or while engaging with life mapping so far? How can you purify your consciousness to gain passage from your Threshold Guardians, so you can proceed to the next stage of your Journey?)

Chapter 4 TOOLS

Your Life Path Portfolio

IV:1 My Life Theme Roles and Qualities
What are some positive and negative or challenging traits that you associate with your Life Themes as recurring kinds of situations and events in your life? (Use the format shown below in your Journal or complete this exercise in your *Life Path Maps Portfolio Toolkit.*)

Life Theme	Positive Qualities	Challenging Qualities
Example: *Education*	*knowledge, skills*	*mere academic, rigid theories*

_____ _____ _____

_____ _____ _____

IV:2 Associating Universal Archetype traits with my Life Themes
For each of your Life Themes, reflect on the table of the Twelve Universal Archetype character traits (repeated below). Associate each of your Life Themes with one or more of the Twelve Universal Archetype personas, based EITHER on their positive traits (i.e., Mission or positive Qualities in the table) OR based on their negative traits (Shadow qualities). You may also refer to Debra J. Breazzano's appendix at the back of this book for more detailed descriptions of each of these Archetype modes.

Life Theme	Archetype Association	Qualities
Example: *Education*	*TEACHER*	*Imparts awareness, Expansive mind*

_____ _____ _____

_____ _____ _____

The Twelve Universal Archetypes

		Mission	Shadow	Qualities
Earth	**Elder Leader**	Provides structure, leadership, authority	Judgmental, strict, critical	Linear thinking, status quo-based
	Artist	To beautify the world, giving form to spirit	Stubborn, passive-aggressive	Earthy, creatively inspired
	Healer	Healing spiritually or physically	Can be codependent caregiver	Sensitive, delicate, ritualistic
Air	**Lover**	To create transcendent partnership	Conflicted over relationship	Commitment to relationship
	Idealist	Help humanity, attain freedom	Rigid about ideals if denied	Visionary, far-reaching mind, intuitive
	Communicator	To link, be messenger	Chatterbox or silent treatment	Synthesizing, curious
Fire	**Warrior**	To pioneer, change	Aggressive or tactless	Fiery, assertive; loves challenge
	Golden Child	Heartful, charismatic, inspirational ruler	Needy, spoiled, arrogant	Draws loyalty, generous, dependable
	Teacher	Impart awareness, learn lessons	Perpetual student, argumentative	Expansive mind, traveler to learn

Water	Nourisher	Nurture of family, community, self	Selfish or martyrdom	Like Ocean, full, nurturing
	Descender	Embracing hardship, leading to growth	Controlling, fearful, depressed, stuck	Deep, intense, private, secretive
	Mystic	Redemption, revelation, wisdom	Addiction and boundary issues	Metaphysical, dreamy, empathetic

IV:3 Archeme-associated Life Theme trends
Journal: Which of the Archetypes that you have associated with your Life Themes (*Tool #IV:2*) are mainly positive, occurring with Life Themes whose impacts you have charted mainly above the neutral Age Line? Which of the Archetypes you have associated with your Life Themes are mainly negative, relating to events you have charted usually below the neutral Age line? Which tend to oscillate? Journal about and describe these trends.

IV:4 Identifying binary, dynamically tense Life Themes associated with internally conflicting Archemes
Consider those Archemes (*Archeme* = Archetype + Life Theme) that you have identified specifically in relation to Life Themes you have mapped, if any, with simultaneously (+5/-5) or other binary, "dynamic tensor" events on your Life Themes Map (*Tool #II:6*). For example, perhaps you associate TEACHER with positive impacts of *Education* Theme events, while at the same time you associate DESCENDER with more negative aspects of some of these same *Education* events.

Life Theme	Positive Archeme	Negative Archeme
Example: *Education*	TEACHER (+5)	DESCENDER (-5)

> (re *Education* #8 event: I was called to the front of class and criticized for poor penmanship in 3rd grade: +5, for the Lesson; -5, socially shamed)

_____ _____ _____

_____ _____ _____

IV:5 What distinctive Life Theme trends occur within the Life Chapters of my Life Story Map?

Example: *Education* is always a +5 factor, showing a "lifting" trend overall, while *Romance* is dynamically tense through chapters 3–5, vacillating between extreme Highs and Lows.

IV:6 My Archemes Map

Mapping: Copy and paste your Life Story Map from chapter 3, *Tool #III:5* into a new page of your Life Path Maps Journal or into the space provided in your *Life Path Maps Portfolio Toolkit* for *Tool# IV:6*. Write in—or insert text if you are using an Excel chart—names of your Archemes (from the Twelve Universal Archetypes table; e.g., LOVER, ELDER LEADER, etc.) onto your Life Story Map. Place your Archeme names onto the Map where the Life Themes with which you are associating them are prominent (i.e., for positive impacts, insert your Archeme name above the Age Line; for negative impacts, insert your Archeme name below the Age Line).

IV:7 My Threshold Guardians

Journal: Have you had threatening or boundary-guarding sorts of animals or human figures show up in your dreams? Can you recognize any specific fears or hesitations about proceeding further in your life-mapping adventure? Wouldn't it be easier to be content with where you are Now, with your newly achieved Threshold vantage point? Journal about how your hesitations or dream barriers may be Threshold Guardians.

IV:8 How might I purify my consciousness to gain passage from my Threshold Guardians?

Journal: Respond to the above prompt in your Journal or in the space provided with this *Tool* in your *Life Path Maps Portfolio Toolkit.*

Chapter 5

LIFE IS . . . DESCENT AND RE-EMERGENCE: CROSS A THRESHOLD TO EMBARK ON YOUR GREATEST ADVENTURE

This chapter's *Tools* conduct you through a Descent passage in your life-mapping odyssey. For you to genuinely Cross the Threshold to *Live Your Dream, Now!* it is not enough to retrace where you have been in your life so far, though that is a big first step that has brought you to your present vantage point as a Dweller at the Threshold. You are ready next to "go the way of the waters," meaning that you may dive into and explore the depths of your memories and commune with facets of your unconscious archetypal impulses so you can gather and reassemble your Strengths for fulfilling your Mission ahead. You will encounter both Dragons and Allies, each of which you can enlist to assist you in fulfilling your Quest.

Descent is a necessary experience in each of our lives sometimes. Consider how the English language uses a vocabulary of Descent to frame a search for truth, understanding, and inner clarity, via phrases such as the following:

Let's get down to the bottom of things.
Go deeper!
Dig in!
I need some down time to consider the situation.

It's hiding just beneath the surface.
. . . the underlying truth

We say we are "down" when we are feeling "depressed." We want to "dive" or "plunge into the depths" of a situation that confounds or confuses our understanding. So, what is all this Down talk about?

The archetypal psychotherapists Carl Jung and James Hillman both described the personal as well as the universal collective unconscious as realms of experience metaphorically beneath the surface of our conscious ego-awareness. These domains of the psyche are the source of our nagging impulses and inner nudges that we *sense* but often find it difficult to "bring up to the surface" directly.

We may "drop" or "sink" into the netherworld of the personal unconscious—and deeper at times into the unfathomable depths of the universal collective unconscious—in our nightly dreams or daydreams. Here our inner ensemble cast of archetypal character modes are able to interact and communicate with us—if we let them—about their unmet needs and helpful insights. Here also in the shadowy underworld of our personal unconscious we can play out our fantasies and troubleshoot interpersonal relations; or, we can also soar upwards into the Heavens, into the heights of our spiritual aspirations with visionary dreams of flight and exploration. Yet it is in the deeper, darker regions of our personal unconscious dreamscapes or imaginative fantasies that we might face our Dragons and encounter the Shadows of our unfulfilled or unintegrated archetypal personas.

> Complete *Tool #V:1* before continuing.
> (Creatively envision and place images within a Cave
> that represent your challenges or Dragons.)

Confronting Your Dragons

Have you encountered recurring images or characters that dog your footsteps in nightly dreams? Have you tried to fathom what it is they represent? Jung found through his longtime personal exploration of dreams that when we do not "own" some archetypal aspect of our psyche it will show up in our dreams—and often in our outward lives as well—as "shadows" or projected images. Jung recognized a Shadow Archetype, and some other archetypal psychologists have observed that any Archetype image may contain both positive as well as negative or repressed Shadow traits.

Recurring Animal images that appear in your dreams may represent traits of Power if they are aggressive, or other qualities from which you wish you could distance yourself or should not embody, although secretly you might desire to express these traits in some form. Frustrating life situations find their way into your shadowy dreams, often in connection with unacknowledged longings.

Joseph Campbell, who wrote about how mythological figures might appear in our dreams, explained that any of us might have inner Dragons that we must consciously confront and "slay"—though I prefer to say, tame—in order to proceed with our innermost callings to achieve our highest potentials.

Your Dragons are shadowy archetypal complexes that impose artificial limits or boundaries on your abilities and inhibit your ambitions. For instance, someone with a lifetime dream of ballet dancing which he has shied away from pursuing might have an unconscious Dragon lurking in the shadows, holding his ambitions in check with negative self-talk: "I could never be a ballet dancer; I am too old/ too young, too heavy/ too skinny!" or, "What would people say?" This sort of inhibiting, "little self" ego-Dragon is also a kind of Threshold Guardian, potentially holding you back from venturing forth to embrace and fulfill your true talents.

Archetypal Dragons and other shadowy unconscious images represent what can feel like insurmountable barriers. They foster fears that inhibit you from actively pursuing your Life Dream; they may do this mainly to protect you from feelings of disillusionment, social shame, or defeat.

To break free from the constraining pinions of your inner Dragons and other shadowy, self-limiting unconscious energies, it is helpful to begin by identifying which sorts of negative thoughts and images serve to trigger your "gut" reactions of fear, inhibition, or frustration.

One of my own inner Dragons used to prompt feelings of personal failure in response to harsh criticism or rejection. I would head for the covers—literally bedcovers, darkened rooms, or whatever reclusive space was available. My scurrying behavior was a Shadow-IDEALIST and DESCENDER reaction to a Shadow-ELDER LEADER figure that dogged my footsteps. It stemmed from my reaction as a child to an easily angered, overly harsh father. When confronted by his anger I would feel the need to Descend and "re-group" in a protective shell of silence and darkness before I could frame a more balanced perspective that would allow me to re-emerge from my comforting cave.

I associate my into-the-shell, unconscious Descent impulse with a long-recurring series of dream images that traces back to as far as six years old with the earliest significant dream that I remember. In the dream, I am returning home from elementary school. (Please note: it can be helpful to use first person, present tense while recalling or reporting on your dreams, because it places you back into the dream more immediately.) I see a male Gorilla reading a comic book, leaning against a corner mailbox across the street from my family's house. I admire the Gorilla's strength and beauty, yet when I get inside the house I immediately run upstairs and hide under my bed-covers, pretending to be asleep, because I fear the Gorilla will come after me. And then he does. The Gorilla takes a sharp knife from a kitchen drawer and climbs up the stairs after me, before placing the knife at my throat.

I awake from this dream, screaming!

In adult years my shadowy Gorilla figure took on a variety of other stock animal forms in my dreams, usually a male Bengal Tiger or a Mother Bear, and occasionally either a male or female Lion. ("Oh, My!" So Dorothy might say!)

In these dreams, I always admire the Animal's powerful, graceful strength. I initially befriend the Tiger, or I come upon a cute Bear Cub in a clearing while walking in the woods with my younger sister before realizing its protective Mother Bear will not be far away. As the dream unfolds, I intuitively know that due to its wild nature, the powerful Animal could be inclined to chase after and overcome me, and after this realization it usually does start to pursue me. I run from the Animal then, either up several levels (e.g., climbing a pine tree to get away from Mother Bear) or through always three degrees of increasingly thick fences or boundaries to escape from the ferocious Tiger.

More recent dreams with these animal images—that is, with their Shadow-ELDER LEADER or Shadow-WARRIOR energies—have shifted in terms of how I am able to respond to their presence in my dream, following several years of dream journaling and dream-centered, archetypal psychotherapy.

Several years ago, for instance, I engaged in an active contemplation following a typical Mother Bear dream. In the dream, my younger sister and I are walking through a clearing in the woods when we see and kneel to cuddle a cute little Bear Cub. Mother Bear soon comes after us to protect her cub. I tell my sister to run and climb up a pine tree just ahead of us, then I climb up after her. I look down as I am climbing and feel a deep admiration as I watch the graceful, powerful Mother Bear climbing up the tree after me just as easily as if she were loping on level land.

This dream lingered in my consciousness, nagging at me. In an active imagination form of contemplation two days later, I asked inwardly for guidance to help me interpret my dream. The dream replayed in my mind's eye entirely, like a video replay clip. Then I received a clear explanation from what I understood to be an inner spiritual Guide.

My Guide stated cogently:

Even though you run from Her, She is pushing you to greater heights!

Reflecting on this message I realized that climbing the pine tree, which is symbolically an *axis mundi* or Tree of Life/ Axis of the World image, represented a positive Ascent to achieve a higher viewpoint, just as my inner Guide had explained.

I realized then that my entire recurring dream complex with the Gorilla and later with Tigers, Lions, and Bears indicated my tendency to project my inherent personal vitality and strength onto others, from fear of wielding it as a potentially dangerous, aggressive force of dominating "Power." I ran from this powerful Other energy in my dreams much as I would "turn tail" from external ELDER LEADER authority figures' biting criticism or rejection.

Complete *Tools #V:2–3* before continuing. (Journal about your own recurring Shadow or Animal dream figures.)

Since I have come to understand and work with these animalistic power-projection dreams, I have eventually been able to assimilate their energies. I have become more capable to "own my own power."

My dreams have shifted dramatically in ways that reflect this change in consciousness. For example, one of my more recent Mother Bear dreams begins with me wandering, alone this time, again in a wooded area. I sense there are probably Bears about (and I say so aloud, aware that my inner Guide is with me), and sure enough, when I look over a ledge down to a lake I see a Mother Bear by the lake with her Cub. Both then start up the hill to get to me.

I climb a large pine tree, quite easily this time. Yet this time as I approach the crest of the *axis mundi*, I arrive at a wooden platform that I walk across, into a scientist's laboratory! A female chemist working there alone hands me a vial with a potion to drink. She says, "Drink this and you will know what to do."

Drinking the potion makes me aware of how best to encounter the Bear. I walk back across the platform to the crest of the pine tree and look down to see first the Bear Cub, followed by Mother Bear, climbing up the tree to come get me. I deftly strip a small piece of bark from the tree, take aim, and drop the bark chip so that, first, it gently knocks the Cub off from the tree to the ground below. I then strip a larger piece of bark and drop it so that it strikes Mother Bear on her forehead; she also drops to the ground and runs off.

I have since wondered, is my bark greater than their bite? Throughout the dream I remained in an inquisitive, self-confident mode; I was not afraid.

As my Bear dream series illustrates, recurring archetypal dream images and situations can certainly change over time. They will transform in a positive manner so long as you take them seriously and actively apply their lessons by modifying your conscious, waking life attitudes and behavior.

> Complete *Tool #V:4* before continuing. (How have changes in your recurring dream scenarios reflected your own changes in attitude or strengths over time?)

Learn to interpret and apply dream lessons in your everyday life. Especially observe your recurring dream images and pay attention to any negative "Dragon-talk," even—perhaps especially!—when it occurs as a waking dream in your outer as life, when your own conscience or other people present negative, limiting statements about your endeavors. As you come to better understand and to actively respond to your dreams or daily triggering events, your dreams will become clearer and more positive while your outer life unfolds as well with greater self-growth and development.

Active Imagination and Journaling as Modes of Descent

Many of the patterns we establish with our conscious attitudes and through our unconscious archetypal outlooks are of our own doing and choice. But some of the more difficult or traumatic situations in life are harder to deal with in this respect: we feel we had no choice in how these situations or patterns came about.

Such memories can inhibit us in the present from venturing forth in certain life situations because we may unconsciously fear that the same sorts of traumatic events could reoccur. Parents divorce or one or both of them die, or a child experiences abuse or health problems from a young age. The child did nothing to cause the stressful circumstances, yet reactive feelings could dog their footsteps for a lifetime.

Traumatic situations can deeply impair our human capacity to trust or to have faith in our natural talents and choices. The trauma may lodge in memory along with unconscious, Archeme-grounded attitudes or Dragon-talk, so that whenever an even slightly similar set of conditions occurs, we are prone to react with fear, avoidance, a sense of helplessness, or dread.

"Re-Vision a Past Event" (*Tool #V:5*) is an active imagination technique that you can use to revisit, from your more aware current perspective, some difficult, significant Shaping Event from the past in which you felt helpless or not in control. By reimagining this early, challenging event from the more mature, safe vantage point of your adult awareness, you can effectively reenvision and reframe the scenario according to "what might have happened differently." This may help you to respond more effectively and with greater awareness when something of a similar nature happens from this point forward.

As an illustration of how you could benefit from this act of Re-Visioning a Past Event (*Tool #V:5*), allow me to share a personal example. When I was in my teens during the radical 1960s, I had a tense relationship with my conservative-minded father. His volatile temper that he often directed at me was beyond my comprehension and my capacity to control.

This came to a head one terrible evening in an encounter from which I felt emotionally scarred and stymied for many years to come. In front of the whole family, next to our dinner alcove table, my father struck me with the back of his hand against my cheek and knocked me to the kitchen floor, because I supported something my brother had said about his own college football team for which my father had berated him.

Nobody came to my aid. Dad sent me off to my room after a demoralizing verbal lashing, with threats of more physical punishment to come.

I remember going downstairs to see my father the next day after being confined to my room all night. No one else was home, and he was sitting in the kitchen alcove. I apologized to him, basically for my having been born to become such a terrible person that he would feel the need to punish me so harshly and so often.

This apology took my father off guard. His jaw dropped; Dad didn't know how to respond. He never raised a hand to me again from that day forward. Yet, I lived with the double memory of his abuse and the abnegation of my own integrity in order to emotionally survive.

I have used the Re-Vision a Past Event technique (*Tool #V:5*) to confront and resolve this painful memory. Adopting a present tense, first–person viewpoint, I closed my eyes and visualized myself back in that crucial scenario with my family, sitting around the dinner alcove. I replayed the memory visually in my mind's eye, re-viewing the entire experience through to the following morning as I was "grounded" in my room. Holding this vantage point, I let myself feel as I had felt back then. Next I journaled, composing an active, as-if-present tense dialogue between myself and my father, allowing each of us to express our heart-to-heart understanding about what had "just" transpired between us.

In this active imagination dialogue, my father and I were each able to express to each other clearly why we had acted and reacted as we did. I was able to hear my father's sincere explanation and his apology for the hurt his actions had caused; and I envisioned him hearing me deeply, too. We forgave each other.

Ever since writing out this active dialogue with this image of my father (ELDER LEADER), I can honestly report that I feel this memory has been permanently healed, and sealed with a new awareness. Now when I recall the original scenario, I remember my later dialogue with Dad as well, and I am thankful that we have resolved what transpired.

In order for you to fully embrace and accept your capacity to claim and to achieve your Life Dream, it is important that you move past the fears, emotional blocks, and inhibitions you have stored in your unconscious memory banks.

You are not helpless in your adult life. You have a capacity for Response-Ability: the capability to respond, not simply to react in habitual ways, to challenging situations. You can reframe and re-envision the Present and the Future as well as events from the Past. You have the freedom to choose how you will act in your current relationships as well as in relation to any opportunity you wish to pursue.

Complete *Tool #V:5* before continuing. (Revisit and resolve a troubling memory with the Re-Vision a Past Event technique.)

Descent—whether occurring in your dreams or via intentional, active imagination—is a fundamental, vital function of a healthy relationship with your Self. However you undertake to engage with troubling memories or shadowy figures of your so-called Dark side, your explorations into landscapes of your dynamic underworld can ironically serve to raise up strengths and awareness that you can use to carry boldly forward.

Rather than hiding your negative feelings or your Archeme-grounded, impulsive attitudes under some musty, proverbial rug, transform and enlist these energies to embark upon a magic carpet ride—one that elevates you to higher awareness so you can manifest your most worthy goals.

You have an inherent capacity to convert even the most daunting of obstacles into golden opportunities for further growth and development. You need only to complete the transformational stage of your life-mapping journey, which begins, ironically as it might at first appear, with your Descent.

Archetype Dialogue Practice

> The process of becoming whole is one by which the psyche strives to incorporate all twelve faces of consciousness into a harmonious blend. –Charles Bebeau & Nin Bebeau, *Archetypes of Soul (Soul Matrix)*, Vol. 2, CreateSpace, 2015

One way to deepen your unconscious wellspring of hidden potentials is by communicating directly with and actively encountering members of your mythic ensemble cast of Archemes. Your Archeme Map (*Tool #IV:6*) identifies the cast of situational identity character guises or role-based persona outlooks that you associate with your Life Themes. Some of your situational, parts-of-Self outlooks contribute a supportive, strengthening influence on your day-to-day choices and attitudes, while others might be critical and could inhibit you from venturing forth to achieve your ambitions.

At the beginning of Dorothy's journey of individuation in *The Wizard of Oz*, the archetypal figures of Scarecrow, Cowardly Lion, and Tin Man each personify unconscious aspects of Dorothy's own character weaknesses. Once Dorothy encounters these undeveloped parts-of-Self directly, they each strengthen their distinctive character traits. Eventually, they orchestrate in unison, under *animus* Toto's lead, to "rescue" Dorothy from her Shadow-ELDER LEADER, Shadow-WARRIOR, and Shadow-NURTURER fears, resulting in a stronger archetypal integration within Dorothy's Total Self System.

Collaborating as an integrated ensemble cast, Dorothy's Archeme Allies empower her to stand with maturity in her individuated Self so she can exercise greater potency and self-awareness. To accomplish this higher self-awareness and integration, Dorothy needed to traverse the Rainbow to her unconscious, topsy-turvy world of Munchkins, Witches, a Forbidden Forest, and a charlatan Wizard in order to encounter and befriend her inner Archemes face-to-face, to call upon each of them to heal and develop their individual Strengths and then to combine them.

Carl Jung's groundbreaking personal exploration of "Archetypes of the collective unconscious" informed his approach to depth or analytical psychology. He encountered firsthand that about which he wrote. During a self-initiated Descent phase for nineteen consecutive evenings and then for over twenty years thereafter more intermittently, Jung put aside an hour or more to engage in what he called active imagination.

Jung isolated himself in a quiet, semi-darkened room. He closed his eyes and allowed himself to sink into a reverie, sometimes imagining himself descending a flight of stairs or entering a shadowy, subterranean realm.

Jung actively invoked archetypal figures of his personal unconscious psyche to communicate and interact with him in their own unconscious domains during his active imagination sessions. Following every dreamlike archetypal encounter, Jung resurfaced and carefully documented these encounters in a special journal, which he named his Black Book. Jung later embellished these accounts and added his own colorful illustrations in what was to become his posthumously published *The Red Book* (C. G. Jung, edited by Sonu Shamdasani et. al., W. W. Norton & Co., 2010).

Jung created profound, colorful Mandala images to represent the life lessons he came to understand following every major encounter with his archetypal cast members during his active imagination-induced visions.

Jung's own ensemble cast of persona Archetype characters included a DESCENDER (Mephistopheles), a MYSTIC with a deep philosophical bent (Philemon), some scholarly TEACHER images, and feminine *anima* figures including a LOVER/Temptress figure and a more matronly, salt-of-the-earth NOURISHER.

In Jung's psychotherapy practice, after his own Descent phase during which he journaled about the encounters with his Archetype personas, Jung encouraged his clients to establish their own active imagination–based, Archetype Dialogue journals.

Archetypal psychologists generally also encourage their clients to undertake dream work along with some form of archetypal identification and Archetype Dialogue. For the next phase of your life-mapping adventure into Descent, I invite you to use this chapter's *Tools #V:6, 8, and 10* to initiate your own Archetype Dialogue Practice.

Begin this journaling practice in your Portfolio journal or in pages provided within your *Life Path Maps Portfolio Toolkit.* I encourage you to also establish a separate Archetype Dialogue journal so you can continue with this journaling process indefinitely. It may be beneficial for you to continue with an ongoing Archetype Dialogue Practice long after you complete your life-mapping odyssey with this book.

The Archetype Dialogue Practice is a self-contained, seven-step process. These seven steps of the Archetype Dialogue Practice are presented gradually for you beginning with this chapter's *Tools #V:6, 8, and 10* and they proceed further with additional *Tools* included with chapters 6 and 9.

I have adapted the seven–step Archetype Dialogue Practice from a standard sort of psychotherapeutic approach employed with cases of Multiple Personality Syndrome (MPS). Psychologists such as William James in the 1890s, along with many current archetypal psychologists, have observed how—in a very normal way—we are "inherently multiple." That is the basis for the awareness that we each naturally house unconscious persona-Archetype character modes, including our situational Archemes, amongst other archetypal images we might also develop in the first place.

People tend to compartmentalize attitudes and to suppress some of their behavioral tendencies or dynamic impulses brewing within their personal unconscious domain. It can be helpful to become consciously aware of and to meet and greet particularly your Archemes, which are those specific Archetype figures you have identified with your situational, dominant Life Themes.

The Archetype Dialogue Practice will allow your Archemes to introduce themselves to each other and to you, within your Total Self System in which you remain the central protagonist as your core, conscious Self. The Archetype Dialogue Practice can equip you to engage directly with and ultimately to enlist and collaborate with your own ensemble cast of primary Archeme Allies. This practice can open channels of communication between your conscious and unconscious outlooks that can integrate and establish greater harmony and balance within your Total Self System, transforming your everyday awareness in a natural way.

The Archetype Dialogue Practice comprises seven steps. It is helpful to complete all seven of these steps according to the processual sequence by which I present them below. The entire process of completing the full seven steps of the Archetype Dialogue Practice, especially for your first time through the process, may take you anywhere from several days to several weeks. I encourage you to take your time with this active imagination and journaling process. Remain with each step until you feel, over one or several Archetype Dialogue sessions, that you have listened to and reported statements in your journal for all of your Archemes who choose to express themselves.

Step One: Meet and Greet Your Archemes (Tool #V:6)

This is the opening phase of the Archetype Dialogue Practice during which you may invite Archeme self-introductions. It is important for your Archemes to get to know one another—and for you to be able to identify and include each of them—as members of your ensemble Archeme cast.

Step Two: Open Mike (Tool #V:8)

During the second phase of Archetype Dialogue Practice, set forth one or more personal discussion topics and invite your Archemes to express their particular viewpoints in an open, conversational mode. The topics you will present to what you may begin to address as your Archeme Allies Council at this stage are general. This step can better familiarize you with the diverse outlooks and values of your internal Archeme cast.

Step Three: Dynamic Archetype Dialogue (Tool #V:10)

For the third phase of your Archetype Dialogue Practice, you are encouraged to engage a "binary event" pair of your dynamically tense Archemes in a dialogue with each other framed around some long-standing conflict in your life. The objective of this exchange will be to expose some of your most polarized internal Archeme viewpoints, so you can better appreciate their influences upon your internal conflicts. As an example, when I invited my Shadow-LOVER Archeme to dialogue with my inner MYSTIC about an emotional conflict I have harbored since childhood, they expressed polar-opposite postulates: "I will never be loved; I am always loved." We may all house some polarized Archeme viewpoints holding to dynamically different grounds within our psyche; these may account for some of our internally conflicting perspectives or values.

Step Four: Individual Archeme Goals (Tool #VI:2)

In the fourth phase of Archetype Dialogue Practice, invite each of your Archemes to share within your Total Self System about their individual goals. What would they like to see You—as the Total Self System they are included within—do or accomplish? What would help each of them individually to feel settled, happy, and fulfilled? This stage can help to illuminate your own diverse goals and "mixed feelings."

Step Five: Establish a Shared, Total Self System Goal to Forge an Archeme Allies Council (Tool #VI:5)

For the sixth phase of your Archetype Dialogue Practice, invite your Archemes to come into closer alignment with one another by identifying, along with your own conscious input, a shared goal or Life Dream that could fulfill your Total Self System. With this phase, enlist your Archemes to agree to serve together as your Archeme Allies Council. The image of King Arthur's Roundtable is relevant at this stage. One-for-All and All-for-One is a contract you may forge with your Archeme Allies Council so that you will manifest your highly integrative, Self-fulfilling Life Dream.

Step Six: Gathering Archeme Ally Mission Contracts (Tool #VI:7)

Once you have established your Archeme Allies Council to assist you to actualize your shared Life Dream, request each Archeme Ally to announce to the Total Self System what qualities they specifically will be able to contribute to help manifest your Life Dream. From this stage forward you may begin to consciously combine and harness the Strengths of your Archeme Allies as your integrated, uniquely individuated Self.

Step Seven: Checking In with your Archeme Allies Council via Your Archetype Dialogue Journal (Tool #IX:4)

After completing your life-mapping odyssey with this book's *Tools*, continue to check in as needed or as desired with members of your Archeme Allies Council. I recommend in chapter 9 for you to establish, if you have not already, an Archetype Dialogue Journal that you can develop and dynamically engage with from this time forward.

I strongly recommend for you to engage the Archetype Dialogue Practice fully, proceeding through all seven steps in the order presented via the *Tools* provided with this chapter and with chapters 6 and 9. Take whatever time feels comfortable to you with each step before you proceed to the next one. This practice can link you with your ensemble cast of Archeme Allies in a way that infuses your awareness every day as a more balanced and integrated, individuated Self.

Alternative Pathways: Meet and Greet Your Archemes, or Explore Your Life Themes?

Guardians of the Threshold may attempt to intercede at this phase, leading some of you who have come this far to hesitate if you are unfamiliar with or if you feel uncomfortable for your own reasons with the notion of identifying and engaging with "unconscious, archetypal parts of Self." Because of this possibility, please allow me to offer here what can be just as effective as an alternative pathway for reflecting on your own inherent dynamism, based on exploring your Life Themes.

For steps one through five of the Archetype Dialogue Practice that I have introduced in the sections above and will elaborate upon further below, you might choose to reflect and journal directly about your Life Themes instead of encountering your Archemes. Some of you may find it useful to practice both approaches with some or all of the seven steps, for your maximal benefit.

Electing the option to reflect on your Life Themes rather than engaging with your unconscious Archeme perspectives might be especially appropriate for any reader diagnosed or at all concerned about potential schizophrenic or borderline personality dispositions, or "voices."

Archemes are not these sorts of voices or impulses. As this book is presenting, Archemes are simply the internalized role identity personas you have developed in relation to those situational sorts of Life Themes that you identified with chapter 2 *Tools.* However, if you embark upon any phase of the seven–step Archetype Dialogue Practice and begin to feel at all that you are connecting with any form of energy or entity that is "not You," I absolutely advise and encourage you to terminate your active imagination session immediately. Then I would encourage you to continue with the alternate *Tools* provided for each of the seven steps so you can reflect directly on insights based on your Life Themes instead of connecting with your Archemes from that point forward.

Please, do not interpret or consider these life-mapping procedures to constitute a psychotherapeutic program. I am, as the author of this book, a cultural anthropologist, not a professional psychologist. I do aim for and have often witnessed these life-mapping activities to facilitate positive, healthful outcomes, which could be therapeutic for you personally. I would recommend for you to seek a professional psychotherapist or psychiatrist for treatment or consultation about any conditions that involve your mental health. Archetypal psychotherapy is one branch of counseling available.

So now, let's get you started with the first three steps of your Archetype Dialogue Practice—or optionally, with your Life Themes Exploration reflections.

Archetype Dialogue Practice/ Life Themes Exploration, Step One: Meet and Greet Your Archeme Cast and/or Explore Qualities of Your Life Themes

For the first step of the Archetype Dialogue Practice (*Tool #V:6*), enter into an active imagination, contemplative state and invite your Archeme personas to step forward and introduce themselves to You and to one another. Engage in an imaginative encounter with members of your Archeme cast, coupled with or followed by journaling about the dialogue that transpires. It is important for you to record this dynamic, internal conversation with your various Archeme parts-of-Self as much "live" or "in person" as you can.

To initiate your active imagination session, establish a quiet, private space where you will not be disturbed for at least thirty minutes to an hour. Turning off your cell phone and other electronic devices, and closing your door with a polite sign taped outside so that family members will know not to disturb you, will help you to focus your attention without interruptions. You may prepare by setting up the room you will use as a special space for your Archetype dialogue sessions in any way you choose, or simply sit in a comfortable recliner, or lie down on a sofa if you prefer, in a softly lit, quiet space. Close your eyes to enter an actively aware, contemplative repose.

Allow your consciousness to "sink" into a state of aware repose. State aloud or silently a simple invitation, such as:

"I invite my Archetypes to come forth and to speak in safety."

Breathe comfortably and focus inwardly while maintaining an attentive, listening mode. To use your active imagination, envision and attend to the conversation with your personified Archeme sub-selves in whatever sort of scene may present itself in your imagination. To use direct Archetype Dialogue journaling, once an archetypal persona has made a connection in your consciousness, you may wish to open your eyes, place pen to paper, and be a recorder as well as a participant in the conversation as it transpires.

Invite your Archemes—or any other of your usually unconscious, archetypal parts-of-Self—who wish to do so, to introduce themselves. Inform them this dialogue is to be a "safe space." Explain that a guideline for Archetype Dialogue is that any persona of your Self, including your own conscious perspective and voice, is welcome to say as much or as little as they choose. Request for there to be no interruptions of one another, and ask for there to be no judgments expressed about whatever is shared in these internal, private conversations.

Announce to your Archemes that the purpose of this initial phase of conversation is simply for self-introductions. You will allow those parts-of-Self who come forth to introduce themselves according to their own nature and outlooks, communicating in first person (using "I" or "me"). They might wish to express in their self-introductions who they "are" as a part of your Total Self System, what they like or dislike, and what they might wish for or fear. Some may prefer not to present themselves at all but might be referred to or introduced indirectly by another.

As one archetypal persona after another "speaks up," you will likely feel a subtle shift in voice tone and perspective as the dialogue comes through in your journal writing or directly in your active imagination. This is quite natural and reinforces the validity of your experience.

As you proceed, you may wish to have on hand a list of the Archeme names you have identified on your Archeme Map (*Tool #IV:6*). You might also have available the Twelve Universal Archetypes table from chapter 4 (pgs. 74–75) to refer to. While it is important to connect especially with your situational Archeme characters and to allow them to identify themselves, do not feel limited to your already identified Archemes; others you have not identified in your Archeme Map might step forth to introduce themselves as well.

Allow ample time for each of your archetypal personas who wish to participate in the conversation to express themselves, keeping in mind the caveat to not proceed further at all if any of these energies feels uncomfortable to you or feels as if it is not "of" or does not belong naturally within your own Total Self System.

By inviting each of your Archeme personas to express themselves in his or her own way without interruptions or judgments, you will create an open, receptive space for getting to know these important members of your personal unconscious, ensemble cast. Additionally, this conversation allows your various "parts-of-Self" to get to know and to hear one another more clearly.

This journaling and/or active imagination practice of Meet and Greet your Archetype Cast, as with all of the seven steps of Archetype Dialogue Practice, may transpire either in one session or over several sittings for an indefinite period of time. You will benefit most by continuing with this initial phase until you intuitively feel that all of your archetypal or Archeme cast members who so choose have had ample opportunity to introduce themselves.

Life Themes Exploration, Step 1

As an alternate to establishing an Archetype Dialogue to Meet and Greet your Archemes, *Tool #V:7* invites you instead to explore basic personal qualities of yourself that you can associate with your Life Themes. If you have a Life Theme of *Education*, for instance, what personal qualities have you developed that have arisen from your experiences in school or as a teacher or student?

What role does each of your Life Themes that you have identified in your Life Themes Map (*Tool #II:6*) play in your life overall? Has its Shaping Events had a mostly positive, or negative, or neutral influence in shaping the person you have become?

Exploring the significance of your Life Themes in your life provides you with a better understanding of some of the Ups and Downs you have experienced. Life Themes often appear to have patterns all their own, as the specific situations that give rise to them activate different dimensions of your Self.

Complete *Tool #V:6* **and/or** *7* before continuing. (Meet and Greet members of your Ensemble Archeme Cast, and/or explore personal qualities of your Life Themes.)

Archetype Dialogue Practice/ Life Themes Exploration, Step Two: Open Mike, or, Situational Life Theme Topics

You can refer to the second step of the Archetype Dialogue Practice as "Open Mike." During this mode of journaling and/or active imagination, establish some topics of conversation in advance, allowing also for spontaneity to bring up additional topics during the internal dialogue. Invite any of your archetypal cast to come forth and express themselves—each in their distinctive voices—about one topic after another. You might ask these Archeme or other archetypal aspects to identify themselves as they step forth.

With Open Mike, invite your archetypal sub-selves to chime in on a range of current topics that are meaningful within your Total Self System. Topics are of a general nature and could relate to a pressing situation, a pending decision, or to some upcoming choice or transition in your life—anything about which you or your archetypal cast members might wish to "weigh in upon."

Your Open Mike conversation can illuminate a wide range of your unconscious motivations. Allow your Archeme cast members to express themselves around a set of one or more personally "loaded" topics.

You may discover through your Archetype Dialogues much about your own internal multiplicity of feelings and perspectives. Allow yourself to shift outlooks deeply and freely as diverse Archetype voices emerge, revealing to you their distinctive and sometimes conflicting viewpoints regarding matters of significance in your life overall. Some personas may choose to remain mute, as silent observers identified indirectly by more vocal or visible Archetypes.

You share the vessel of your Total Self System consciousness with a rich panoply of conscious and unconscious personas expressing a wide range of attitudes and viewpoints. The more you accept and embrace each Archeme presence as it expresses itself in terms of feeling and voice within your Archetype Dialogue, the better you will be able to reveal sources of your "mixed feelings" around certain ideas, beliefs, and relationships.

How often, if ever, is anyone truly "of one mind" regarding important matters of the Heart? Once you are able to recognize and establish a collaborative interaction with your usually submerged parts-of-Self, you may call upon your unconscious personas as Allies rather than responding unknowingly to a nebulous range of vague impulses expressing such feelings as anger, frustration, fear, hope, or anxiety.

Your archetypal personas do not need to remain constrained or hidden in your shadowy depths; call upon them to help you illuminate dynamic facets of your mixed perspectives and attitudes.

Life Themes Exploration, Step 2

Tool #V:9 offers an alternative or an additional approach you can use to explore how your own dynamic nature may have developed a wide range of attitudes pertaining to some general topics in your life. Your multiple Life Themes have helped you to develop different role identity outlooks in specific sorts of situations. How do you regard a range of topics that are important to you based on different perspectives you have developed in your various role identities related to each of your Life Themes?

Understanding your own multiple attitudes or feelings that you can associate with the different role identities you have developed in your life can help you understand where you are regarding specific situations or decisions.

Complete *Tools #V:8 and/or 9* before continuing. (Engage in an Open Mike Archetype Dialogue, and/or explore the topical relevance of your Life Themes.)

Archetype Dialogue Practice/ Life Themes Exploration, Step Three: Dynamic Archeme Dialogue, or, Understanding Your Conflicting Role Identities

Step Three of the Archetype Dialogue Practice provides a technique you can use to expose your Dragons—or rather, to invite the Angel and Devil pair sitting on your shoulders to face off over some of your most difficult personal challenges! This journaling and/or active imagination dialogue technique is designed to illuminate some of your most polarized internal motivations and perspectives. After you feel you have adequately explored and tapped, as it were, your Archeme perspectives around several topics for over a week or more with your Step Two Open Mike dialogues, you are ready next to dive more deeply with your Descent by initiating a Dynamic Archetype Dialogue.

To begin this step, make a list of one or more of your most persistent personal conflicts. This may include any issue about which you have frequently felt "torn" or "split." Focus on deep emotional issues or on the kinds of choices you tend to waffle about or vacillate over when it comes to making decisions. Choose one or more of your most difficult conundrums as a topic to carry with you to the bottom-most nadir of your Descent.

To select a dynamic pair of Archeme viewpoints to invite into a polar-opposite form of debate so you can expose issues surrounding your deeply entrenched inner conflicts, review your Shaping Events Record (*Tool #II:3*). Look especially at the Turning Point sorts of events that you have rated on your Life Themes Map (*Tool #II:6*) as "dynamic tensor events." These are Shaping Events you have retrospectively rated with binary impact scores—that is, as having had both positive as well as negative impacts on your life. Were any of these binary Shaping Events so extremely "dynamic" or polarized in their impact that you rated them as at or nearly (+5/-5)? If so, the Archemes you have associated with these events' Life Themes on your Archemes Map (*Tool #IV:6*) are likely to be opposite-quality Archemes.

For example, for a *Relationship* Life Theme with several (+5/-5) impact Shaping Events (such as a divorce, for instance, or several failed relationships), one might have associated LOVER with the positive, (+5) impact of these events but DESCENDER or perhaps Shadow-IDEALIST with the (-5) impact of these same events. It is this sort of opposing, (+5/-5), Archeme pairs that I encourage you to invite via active imagination to engage together in a Dynamic Archetype Dialogue. Propose as a topic to one of your opposed Archeme pairs a recurring, nagging personal conflict that relates to the positive and negative impacts of their shared Life Theme, to which these two Archemes are assigned.

For illustration, consider Mindy's story again from pgs. 78–82. On Mindy's Archeme Map she identified WARRIOR and DESCENDER as two Archeme characters who represent dynamically opposed facets of her Total Self System. Mindy associates these two opposed Archemes with her Life Themes of *Spiritual* and *Physical*, respectively. Mindy rated her *Spiritual*/WARRIOR Shaping Events as having had a consistently positive (+5) impact, while she rated all of her *Physical*/DESCENDER events as having had (-5) negative impacts. As well, all of Mindy's Turning points, which she also rated as (+5/-5), she identified in their positive and negative impacts, respectively, with WARRIOR and DESCENDER Archemes.

Mindy engaged in a journaling–based Dynamic Archetype Dialogue including these polar-opposite WARRIOR and DESCENDER Archemes around a core issue for Mindy of the difficulty she has had in her life for maintaining long-term commitments. Her WARRIOR and DESCENDER Archemes each separately identified a same goal of "freedom" in their dialogue, yet Mindy was surprised to learn from their dialogue that Freedom holds very different meanings for these opposite-pole aspects of her Self.

To Mindy's WARRIOR part-of-Self, Freedom allows her to follow her inner spiritual nudges so she can be flexible and creative in pursuing her options and expressing her personal values. To her DESCENDER Archeme, on the other hand, holding to any one choice or commitment feels confining. Mindy's DESCENDER compels her never to settle for very long in any one career, location, or relationship.

Reflecting on the Dynamic Archetype Dialogue she had journaled from the opposing perspectives of her WARRIOR and DESCENDER Archeme cast members, Mindy recognized her internal conflict around the issue of "freedom" she has established in her life. She realized how she has sometimes mistaken her DESCENDER's nudges for "freedom," based on its dislike of personal commitment, for authentic *Spiritual* "callings." Once she realized this, Mindy encouraged these two Archemes in her dialogue journaling to come to an agreement that would allow Mindy to balance her need for holding to her commitments with her need for "freedom." She has been happily married since shortly after completing her life-mapping process and she continues to live a dynamic, creative, and spiritual life full of travel as well as commitment.

Now then, *Tool #V:10* invites you to present the topic of one or more of your own persistent inner conflicts to a dynamically opposed pair of your own internal Archeme perspectives. Invite these polarized Archemes to discuss this slippery topic between themselves while you mainly observe, and ask questions to stimulate their debate within your journaling and/or active imagination encounter. Allow this practice to continue long enough to reveal clearly the two opposed positions held by these opposed unconscious outlooks and motivations that compete for your attention within your Total Self System.

If you are not sure which conflictual situation to focus on for your Dynamic Archetype Dialogue, make a brief list of some ideas or issues around which you have often felt a strong internal conflict. As a trigger, try making a list of statements that complete the following prompt: {"I will never _____"}. Invite a polar-opposed pair of Archemes from your Archeme Map to engage in a spirited conversation including these Dragon-like forms of negative self-talk. Allow the positive Archeme from this pair to counter such "I will never" statements with opposite, positive self-affirmations: "I will always _____."

Life Themes Exploration, Step 3

Because you have developed somewhat different role identities and outlooks based on the recurring types of situations in your life that you have identified as your Life Themes (*Tool #II:6*), sometimes you may feel deeply conflicted about which way to turn or how to resolve a difficult problem you might face. Some of your Life Themes might have led you to develop even antithetical or opposite outlooks with respect to some underlying issue.

Exploring the influence of your Life Theme-associated role identities with *Tool #V:11* can help you to better understand some of your most persistent internal conflicts or "self-conflicts." As a parent, for example, a role that you might associate with a *Family* Life Theme, you might wish to prevent your daughter from taking a risky adventure, while at the same time your own sense of adventure associated with a *Travel* Theme could be at odds with your parental protectiveness.

You want your daughter to take that trip alone to Paris, but at the same time you don't want to see her take undue risks on such a solo adventure. Exploring your different Life Theme-related outlooks could help you arrive at a compromise between your internally competing outlooks. Maybe you can hire a chaperone in Paris who will accompany your daughter, so she will feel free to venture forth on her adventure without causing you to be in constant worry while she is gone!

> Complete *Tools #V:10 and/or 11* before continuing.
> (Journal a Dynamic Archetype Dialogue, and/or Journal about Lifting and Descending patterns of any of your opposite-influence Life Themes.)

Re-Emergence

The first three stages of Archetype Dialogue Practice and/or Life Themes Exploration presented with this chapter's *Tools* can help you realize the dynamic multiplicity and rich vitality of your Total Self System. Human thoughts, feelings, and motives are often mixed, especially insofar as we suppress archetypal sentiments or are not well attending to them. Archetype Dialogue Practice, or other means of tapping into and listening to your internalized Archeme motivations and viewpoints, can free you—as ironically as it might at first seem—from the tyranny of masked or hidden feelings that might otherwise continue to fester and inhibit your thoughts and behavior without your knowing why.

Unconscious feelings of frustration, dread, or depression could cloud your consciousness to the point that you might no longer seek to pursue goals you were once passionate about fulfilling. Descent can help you recognize the sources of your most persistent, inhibiting thoughts and feelings for what they are: archetypally framed facets of consciousness expressed as unconscious reactions to difficult situations from your past, which no longer need to have their hold on you.

Through personifying and checking in with your ensemble Archeme cast, you can develop a greater compassion for these diverse and vitally important facets of your Self. You can collaborate with these energetic potentials within You as Allies rather than avoiding or seeking to bury them as Dragons or as "enemies within."

Allow me next to take this chapter in another direction with a fresh angle on Descent. Descent is a vital practice for self-exploration and for tuning into your Archemes' "mixed messages" surrounding your internal conflicts and attitudes. As well, though, it is perhaps equally as important to engage in experiences of Ascent as a valuable dimension of your Journey.

Spiritual practices including active contemplation, prayer, or meditation can help you to connect with your Higher Self. These practices can lift you to achieve higher awareness, or Ascent. Internal dialogue through prayer, active contemplation, dream work, and journaling with your inner spiritual agencies or Guides is a good addition to the archetypal work you are engaging with this chapter's *Tools*. Ascent raises your lessons "up" to be assimilated into the fabric of your own higher-consciousness awareness.

Complete *Tool #V:12* before continuing.
(Review and journal about your Descent practices from chapter 5 *Tools*. What have you discovered about your Total Self System? What have you gained?)

Chapter 5 TOOLS

Your Life Path Portfolio

V:1 My Cave Art
Create: Copy or draw a picture of an open, deep Cave in your Life Maps Portfolio Journal (or use the image provided in your *Toolkit* for *Tool #V:1*). Insert computer icons, paste magazine pictures, or draw your own images inside this Cave that symbolically represent your obstacles, fears, or "Dragons" (e.g., recurring dream Animal figures or other "shadowy" objects or forms).

V:2 A Dream Journal Entry
Start a Dream Journal (if you haven't already). Journal about any recurring Shadow or Animal dream images.

V:3 Recurring Shadow or Animal Dream Images
Journal: Contemplate and then journal about the personal meaning of your Shadow or Animal image dreams. What messages do they represent?

V:4 Changing Dream Images Over Time
Journal: Have your recurring Shadow or Animal dream images changed over time? Describe an example below and journal about the reasons you can attribute to these changes.

V:5 Re-Vision a Past Event
Journal: While we cannot directly alter the events of our past, we can change our responses. For a significant Shaping Event of your life that led to an undesirable downturn in your feelings or motivations about life overall, journal about how you might have differently responded to the event, either when it occurred or shortly afterwards, based on your more mature present understanding. Write

in the first person (I, me) viewpoint and use present tense from the vantage point of being back *in* that situation as it is occurring or just following it. Envision and/or write down, as though it is occurring NOW, what you and significant others involved could have said, done, or thought differently that could have affected you from that moment forward more favorably. Note: It is important for you to revise the actual dialogue or actions that occurred within the event; or, journal a dialogue with your significant alter from within the event as if it is soon after the event occurred. Make sure you journal your dialogue with this relevant person (or persons) AS IF you are in real time back then.

V:6 My Archetype Dialogue Practice, Step One: Meet and Greet My Archetypal Ensemble Cast Members

Situate yourself in a comfortable, quiet space. Close your eyes and "sink into" an active contemplation session. Invite your Archemes and any other archetypal aspects that wish to step forward as distinct viewpoints to introduce themselves. Set a ground rule of "safe space": any aspect can speak without judgment or interruption from other perspectives within your Total Self System. You can ask probing questions while you journal the dialogue as it occurs, or else you can inwardly envision the dialogue. (Then, record what you recall from it later.) Introduce questions such as: "Who Are You?" "What do you like? not like? fear? love? hate?, etc. Allow this dialogue to continue over one or more contemplation and journaling sessions, as necessary, until you intuitively sense that all of your Archemes or archetypal personas that wish to have had their opportunity to "Meet and Greet" you and each other.

Archetype Dialogue journaling example:

LW:	*Would anyone like to introduce yourself?*
Arch 1:	*What do you want us to talk about?*
LW:	*Well, who are you, for instance?*
Arch 1:	*You know me as "Little Linda."*
LW:	*Oh! Hello.*

Arch 1:   *I live "down here," you know.*
LW: *May I call you a Descender then?*
Arch 1/ Descender: *Okay . . .*

V:7 *My Life Themes Exploration, Step One:* Strength (positive) and Shadow (negative) personal character qualities that I associate with my Life Themes

What character qualities have you developed in relation to your Life Themes (from your list of Life Themes, *Tool #II:5*), including personal Strengths and/or challenging or negative traits? See the example to format your response, below, or use the format in your *Portfolio Toolkit* for chapter 5, Tool #7.

Life Theme	Positive Character Traits	Negative Character Traits
Example: *Family*	*nurturing tendency*	*runt of family / shyness*
_____	_____	_____
_____	_____	_____

V:8 My Archetype Dialogue Practice, Step Two: Open Mike

Situate yourself in a comfortable, quiet space. Close your eyes and sink into an active contemplation session. Invite your Archemes and other archetypal aspects that wish to step forward to express their distinct viewpoints around one or more topics that are current in your life, such as an upcoming decision or a recent event. Continue this practice over one or more sessions, focusing on one or several topics, until you intuitively sense that you have heard a wide range of characteristic responses or attitudes to various open mike topics within your Total Self System.

V:9 My Life Themes Exploration, Step Two: Relevance of My Life Themes to Current Situations

Journal: Consider one or more current topics in your life. Choose situations that are relevant to two or more of your Life Themes from your list of Life Themes, *Tool #II:5*. Journal about personal viewpoints you hold about these topics from the perspectives of your distinct social identities or roles that you associate with each Life Theme.

V:10 My Archetype Dialogue Practice, Step Three: Dynamic Archeme Dialogue

1. Identify two Archemes from your Archeme Map (*Tool #II:6*) that you have associated with the positive AND negative pole values for one or more Shaping Events that you have rated to have binary impact values (e.g., +5/ -5 for the same event). For example, for a *Romance*-related event, you may have associated LOVER with a +5 value and DESCENDER with a -5 value for the same event on your Life Themes Map.

2. Situate yourself in a comfortable, quiet space. Close your eyes and sink into an active contemplation session. Introduce the topic of a long-standing internal conflict that is relevant to the two opposed Archemes you have identified in the above step with one or more binary events. Present a challenging topic from your life about which of these two Archeme perspectives holds different or even opposite positions or attitudes. Envision and journal a dialogue about your long-standing internal conflict (either during or after your active imagination session) between these two opposed Archeme perspectives. Allow these dynamically opposed perspectives to clearly express their distinctive stances about this topic so that they "hear" each other and you get to see both sides of your internal dynamic around the topic.

V:11 My Life Themes Exploration, Step Three: Exploring My Contrasting Life Theme Patterns

Journal: Review your Life Story Map from *Tool #III:5*. Do one or more of your Life Themes show a pattern of being always positive in their impact ratings? Always negative? Oscillating Up and Down? Neutral (plotted mainly along the "zero rated" Age Line)? Describe the patterns you see evident in your Life Themes. Where two of your Life Themes appear almost diametrically opposed or opposite in the impact value trends, can you think of a current or recent situation where your own attitudes based on experiences around these opposing Themes may have influenced you to have an internal conflict about some decision or action? Journal about the separate influences on your attitudes or thinking based on how you might approach the same event from different perspectives related to these opposing Life Themes. Can you arrive at a compromise that resolves your inner conflict?

V:12 Re-Emergence from Descent: My Life Lessons
Journal: Review your Descent practice creative and journaling entries from this chapter's *Tool* activities (*Tools #V:1-#V:11*). What have you discovered about yourself? What have you learned? Journal about what you can learn from reviewing your Descent activity insights as Life Lessons.

Chapter 6

LIFE IS . . . HEEDING THE CALL: RECLAIM YOUR LIFE DREAM

What do you want to be when you grow up, regardless of your age? Are you doing today what you have always hoped and dreamed you would be doing with your life to this point? If not, how and why have your goals and accomplishments shifted along the way? Certainly your experiences along the carousel ride of a lifetime have affected and may have led you to redirect your life course in subtle and sometimes in dramatic ways.

The situational Themes that shape the warp and weave of your life's focus and ambitions form patterns, as you have discovered with your Life Story Map (*Tool #III:5*). To the extent that your Life Themes with their associated Archeme or role-identity outlooks have infused you with multiple perspectives, it might appear inevitable that these recurring types of situations in your life—along with your typical responses and attitudes—will continue indefinitely. This might bring about *déja vu* feelings regarding your casual routines and a comforting feeling of familiarity with your fixed relations. Yet it could also lead to feelings of frustrating, stubborn sameness with respect to repeating situations in your life from which you might wish you could finally learn and move on.

> Complete *Tool #VI:1* before continuing. (Which Life Themes have been most helpful and which have been most challenging in your life?)

Archetype Dialogue Practice/ Life Themes Exploration, Step Four: Your Individual Archeme and Situational Goals.

To understand your mixed motivations with regard to recurring situations in your life, I invite you to engage with Step Four of the Archetype Dialogue Practice and/or Life Themes Exploration. Consider again how you have associated each of your Life Themes with one or more role-identity Archemes. Step Four of your Archetype Dialogue Practice aims to uncover your goals in relation to each of your Archeme orientations. (Alternately, identify and reflect upon the goals you hold with respect to each of your distinctive Life Themes with *Tool #VI:3.*)

Each of your Archeme energy modes or role-identity outlooks embodies its own motivations and values to some extent, and aims to pursue its own goals. It can be helpful for you to "excavate" or "mine," as it were, each of your Archemes' individual goals. You will then be better equipped to reflect upon how to better integrate your sometimes mixed or divergent goal motivations with a more unified focus. This can help you begin to frame and envision your Life Dream.

For the fourth step of your Archetype Dialogue Practice, again begin by establishing a comfortable, quiet environment to engage in active imagination with your Archemes and other archetypal presences that might come forth. Invite the members of your ensemble Archeme cast to express their unique viewpoints with regard to their own goals. These could include their goals for You—as the Total Self System they are embedded within—from the vantage point of the situational Life Theme roles they represent. Especially when an Archetype persona has felt suppressed, cut off, or inhibited, the goals they express might be highly charged in relation to their specific "buried" needs.

You may serve as an interviewer as well as a recorder for this phase of your Archetype Dialogues. Practice this step over one or more sessions, until you feel that each of your Archeme personas, who wish to, has expressed and clarified their goals.

Keep a record. If you engage with your Archeme cast by direct active imagination prior to journaling the dialogue, be able to identify each Archeme that emerges so you can record the goals he or she has expressed. As with all of your Archetype Dialogues, remember to maintain this conversation as a safe space, without interruption or judgment by You or any of your archetypal sub-selves.

Life Themes Exploration, Step Four

You may have distinct goals regarding each of your recurring Life Themes (from your Life Themes map, *Tool #2:6*). Some of these Life Theme goals may have become high priorities for you, while your goals with some other Life Themes might not be fulfilled or could benefit from your attention. *Tool #VI:3* allows you to identify the goals you have established or that you might like to establish for each of your Life Goals.

> Complete *Tools #VI:2 and/or 3* before continuing (Invite your Archemes to declare their own goals; and/or explore your goals with respect to each of your Life Themes.)

Alternate Future Lifescapes

Now that you have clarified your individual Archeme—or alternately, your individual Life Theme—goals and motivations, I encourage you to envision a set of future life scenarios that could fulfill these goals. Project an "ideal future lifescape" for every Life Theme or Archeme included in your goal statements from the previous step. Or, creatively envision several future lifescape scenarios that would fulfill various combinations of the goals expressed by your ensemble Archeme cast members or your combined Life Themes. I encourage you to visualize and then journal about—and/or, artistically represent—each of these alternate future lifescapes. Creatively map out pathways by which you could arrive at these various future scenarios. Take note of which Archemes goals are being fulfilled by each of your envisioned prospections.

For example, based on my own Archemes' goals from Archetype Dialogue journaling, I have envisioned one of my own possible Alternate Future Lifescapes as follows:

I am living in Ireland {IDEALIST Archeme}, in a cottage near the Western seacoast in County Mayo. I travel regularly to the States as well as to a Life-Mapping Institute that I've established branches of in Galway and in Western New York State. I provide retreat workshops, seminars, and trainings to help people from far and wide to envision and realize their Life Dreams; at this Institute I also train and certify new Life Path Maps coaches {COMMUNICATOR; TEACHER; ELDER LEADER}. I live with my family of beloved pet companions, near to my sisters, and in connection with a community of like-minded friends. We support and help facilitate each other's personal and creative Life Missions {LOVER; NOURISHER; MYSTIC}.

It is important to "future cast" by envisioning not just one but several Alternate Future Lifescapes at this juncture of your life-mapping adventure. Allow your Alternate Future Lifescape envisioning to cover and to fertilize the grounds for all of your Archeme and/or Life Theme aspirations. These Alternate Future Lifescapes, taken together, form a composite view of your Total Self System's future yearnings and unconscious motivations.

> Complete *Tool #VI:4* before continuing.
> (Envision several Alternate Future Lifescapes.)

Your Life Purpose: Core Values and Priorities

Compare the possible pathways you have envisioned to realize your life goals in your Alternate Future Lifescapes (*Tool #VI:4*), looking to identify some common ideas. Which elements of your Alternate Future Lifescapes ring most true to your heart? Which pathways could most fully unfold those potentials you most deeply seek to fulfill?

Why are you here, after all? This is a loaded question. How you answer this question can help you to envision a Future Lifescape worthy of your pursuit. Consider what you aim to fulfill in your life in terms of your core values and ideals, rather than merely your material objectives. This can help you clarify your Life Purpose.

Envision a scenario of life conditions in which you are truly happy. These conditions could manifest core values of yours such as: being loved and loving, expressing generosity, achieving serenity, being compassionate and effective in service to others, having abundant freedom to create, being adventurous, or realizing spiritual fulfillment.

Framing your future life goals in terms of values rather than as specific jobs, locations, or activities will help you to maintain flexibility, allowing for various pathways by which you can fulfill your deepest goals.

Tool #VI:5 guides you to arrive at a statement of your Life Purpose. When you are ready, I invite you to enter this statement into your Portfolio Journal or in the space provided in your *Portfolio Toolkit* for this *Tool*.

Marnie

When a person changes their outlook on their future prospects by orienting to purposive, value-oriented goals, this empowers them to take huge strides in their lives that move them in the direction of fulfilling their deepest potentials. Focusing on the values you associate with your goals, whether long-term or short-term, naturally brings these values more clearly into focus. I have been amazed at how seemingly effortless changes may come into the life of someone who has engaged deeply with life mapping. I assume no credit for this; it is a natural by-product of your own internal tending to your Life Path. By engaging heartfully in a process of life review, reflection, and positive future envisioning, you are planting and nurturing fertile seeds for personal growth and fulfillment.

Visualization is a key factor here. The more clearly envision yourself living the life you choose, the freer you are to conduct yourself—already, today—according to the mind-set of that vision as an emerging scenario.

Marnie is a life mapper who lives in the American Southwest. She undertook life mapping a few years after she lost her life partner to cancer following fifteen years of a deeply fulfilling marriage. She was at a crossroads in her life, not knowing how she could even conceive of a future without her beloved.

Through life mapping, Marnie could recognize in her thematic Life Story the pathway that had brought her to the Threshold where she stood. She had already completed a full Epic-Comic Adventure, through Life Chapters that she named: *Childhood Hell*; *Achieving Graduation* and *Giving Back*. So, what was there left for her to look forward to?

Marnie discovered two strong Archeme Allies within her unconscious cast of persona characters: ELDER LEADER and COMMUNICATOR.

She associated ELDER LEADER with her *Idyllic* Life Theme, while COMMUNICATOR has been dominant during *Wrenching* times. She realized that through coping with hardship she has learned to express herself better, so her *Wrenching* times have imparted valuable life lessons.

From active imagination and journaling dialogues with her ELDER LEADER and COMMUNICATOR Archemes, Marnie came to understand that what she most wanted following the death of her spouse were three things: to establish a closer sense of Family or family-like togetherness, to gain a greater capacity for Freedom, and to further develop her spiritual pursuits.

After identifying Archeme goals and projecting a range of Alternate Future Lifescapes that could allow her to realize the core values implicit with her goals, within a short span of time Marnie's life course took some dramatic turns she could not have anticipated yet which have brought into her life precisely what she has yearned for!

Within a year after completing her life-mapping process, Marnie's daughter—pregnant with Marnie's first grandchild—unexpectedly decided she and her husband would move to within a mile of Marnie's home. She became thereby more engaged on a day-to-day basis with her close family ties. Within eighteen months, the job Marnie had held for nineteen years dissolved due to an economic crunch. She was out of a job—though with six months bonus pay—and she found that with her retirement pension and monthly social security checks, she would not need to depend on having a job for financial survival anymore; she was free!

Not having to work from nine to five to make a living has provided time for Marnie to pursue her third and deepest goal: spiritual service to others ("giving back") and focusing more diligently upon pursuing her spiritual unfoldment.

Marnie now volunteers with the local sheriff's department, counseling family members suddenly bereaved through the accidental or crime-related death of a loved one. Coming full circle, Marnie helps bereaved persons by communicating with others about how one can eventually move on in life after the heavy loss of a loved one. This fulfills her desire to live her own life with a stronger sense of communal Family, too.

Below is Marnie's Life Story Map, embellished with computer clip art icons to represent her critical Turning Points.

Marnie expressed her life goals in terms of core values rather than as concrete objectives: family togetherness, freedom, and spiritual development. She could not have anticipated her daughter's pregnancy or move; her daughter was not even married yet when Marnie undertook life mapping. She certainly would not have asked for her job of nineteen years to dissolve in order to manifest her goals of greater freedom or more time for spiritual activity. Yet after consciously staking claim to her life purpose and goals, it is as if the Universe or divine providence Itself has stepped in to clear her way!

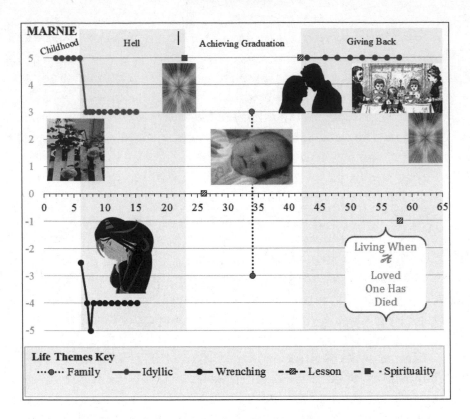

Your Life Mission Statement: What Are You Here For?

Focusing your attention on the values and goals you desire to manifest, as in Marnie's story, can empower you to recognize the abundant gifts of opportunity and possibility that come your way. Losing a job can be a daunting experience, but recognizing the freedom that circumstance brings for you to fulfill your Life Purpose shifts the event to the positive. Life mapping encourages you to clarify your values and goals with a receptive, flexible mind-set.

Stating a Life Purpose is good, yet along with identifying *why* you are here, you can also benefit from forging a Mission Statement to support you in the day-to-day process of actualizing and living your Dream. Like the mission statement of a successful organization, your personal Life Mission Statement provides an action-oriented focus around which you can organize your ideal, value-based lifestyle.

To assure that your Life Mission Statement incorporates your most integrative goals, I invite you to engage in the next step of your Archetype Dialogue Practice/Life Themes Exploration. Invite your Archemes to unite to form an Archeme Allies Council that will collaborate to help you manifest your most fulfilling life goals, those which your Archeme cast of personas share in common with You within your Total Self System.

Archetype Dialogue Practice/ Life Themes Exploration, Step Five: Forming Your Archeme Allies Council

One benefit of Archetype Dialogue Practice is to acquaint yourself with your situationally framed perspectives so you can synthesize and integrate them better within your uniquely individuated, Total Self System. Once focused in this more integrated manner, you will be able to call upon and harness all of your positive Archeme Strengths to help you harness and fulfill your potentials. Archetype Dialogue allows you to come into a more aware, collaborative relationship with members of your ensemble archetypal cast.

Some of your unconscious sub-selves might tend to be in Shadow mode, associated with negative emotional states or projecting self-limiting, Dragon-like postulates because of difficult experiences they are associated with from your situational life history. Ultimately, though, any of the Twelve Universal Archetype character modes also embody powerful Strengths that can help you go after and accomplish your aspirations. This is naturally their most positive function.

With Step Five of Archetype Dialogue Practice, your aim is to recruit and enlist your Archemes cast to come together to form an Archeme Allies Council by helping you claim and clarify a unified Life Mission Statement. Declaring your integrative Life Mission in this manner can empower you to realize your deepest potentials such that, ultimately, your Archeme Allies Council will accompany you every step of the way as you go forth to *Live your Dream, Now!*

Using active imagination and/or a live journaling session, for this level of internal conversation, invite your Archemes—along with any other unconscious personae who might yet emerge at this stage—to help you identify one or more "big" goals which you all agree are vitally important for you to actualize as a Total Self System in the process of fulfilling your Life Mission.

Allow your Archemes to help you recognize some goals that cut across most or even all of your situational Life Theme pursuits. Some of your deepest aspirations may have become "buried" over time as forfeited goals deposited in your Archemes' shadow states, as it were, as an unconscious response to some of your most challenging Life Chapter events. Your situational Archeme Allies can help you Now to retrieve or excavate these buried aspirations.

After you have collectively identified your most integrative goals as a Total Self System based on the formation of your Archeme Allies Council, with Step 5 of your Archetype Dialogue Practice you can also invite your Archemes to step forward individually to offer the specific Strengths they each possess that can assist your Total Self System to realize your Life Mission potentials. Forge an inner agreement and compose a written "Archeme Contract" (*Tool #VI:7*) with each of your Archemes that frames how they will agree to assist you and one another to realize your potentials on a day-to-day basis as you move forward together as a unifed Self to fully realize your Life Mission.

You are forming with Step Five of your Archetype Dialogue Practice a collaborative, mutually nurturing and attentive internal community based on your Total Self integration, much as Dorothy and her archetypal Ally companions formed with their collaborative quest to defeat the Wicked Witch. Each of Dorothy's ensemble Archeme characters strengthened their own natures and achieved their own goals while also helping Dorothy and Toto ultimately return to Kansas (or, to the Conscious domain, as Jean Houston aptly observes in her book, *The Wizard of Us*, Atria, 2012). Acting harmoniously together as Dorothy's Total Self System, they serve the larger potentials of Dorothy's integrative Life Mission; to gain the maturity and personal strengths Dorothy needs to stand in her own shoes (ruby, or of the Heart, of course!) so she can save Toto and in so doing assert positively her own *animus* nature.

If you prefer to work with your Life Themes directly rather than dialoguing with your Archeme parts of Self, simply ask yourself how the goals you have developed with each of your recurring situational Life Themes might intersect around the idea of your own unified or cross-situational Life Mission. How might you incorporate the life lessons and insights you have gained from your Life Story (*Tool #III:5*) within a Life Mission Statement, the fulfillment of which could bring together and harness many or even all of your Life Theme goals?

This level of attainment of Life Theme integration and/or of the formation of your Archeme Allies Council is important for you to achieve in order for you to go forward in greater Strength of character to the realization of your deepest life potentials. I am asking you, now that you have come this far, to never turn back or settle for less! Most people may never even aim to reach this stage because they remain essentially unaware either of their recurring Life Theme threads and complex role identities or of their unconscious repertoire of Archemes with their complex assortment of Strength and Shadow traits. Your Archetype Dialogue encounters and/or your Life Themes Exploration equips you to understand the dynamism of your Total Self System so you can proceed forward to realize your Life Mission from what Carl Jung would call a more integrated, individuated awareness.

Life Themes Exploration, Step 5

Each of your Life Themes involves specific sorts of situations through which you have developed your personal character potentials. Combining these potentials can help you to gather your strengths, so you can face any situation with a more integrated Self.

Tool VI:6 invites you to explore the different facets of your multiple Life Themes so you can appreciate how you have developed somewhat distinct personal character qualities within each of these recurring types of situations. What happens when you conjoin these distinct, thematic personal quality elements within a more unified outlook? This is a process of Self-building whereby you may establish a repertoire of your finest, deepest qualities to draw from more consciously in any situation.

> Complete *Tools #VI:5–7* before continuing. (Forge your Archeme Allies Council; Consider how combining character qualities from your various Life Themes can help you identify your strengths to actualize your Life Mission. Establish Archeme Ally "Mission contracts")

You may arrive at your Life Mission Statement by reflecting on results from your Archeme Allies Council dialogue (*Tool #VI:5*) and/or your Life Theme Integration journaling (*Tool VI:6*). Record your Life Mission Statement in your Portfolio Journal or in your *Portfolio Toolkit*, using *Tool #VI:8*, for later reference.

Goddrick

To illustrate how establishing a Life Mission statement can help you clarify and fulfill your Life Dream, consider Goddrick. Goddrick has had to negotiate the slippery slope of unemployment and underemployment since the US Great Recession of 2008. Goddrick experienced a difficult series of short-term job gains and losses over a period of several years. He sought out life mapping to explore his priorities as he approached yet another job search.

Through his life-mapping "time out," Goddrick came to recognize how his workaday jobs had in recent years not been aligned with his core values. His most recent jobs in the computer tech industry had not provided space for Goddrick's ARTIST and IDEALIST Archeme energies to thrive, so he was internally conflicted and unhappy at work. He realized he was sabotaging himself at these jobs and at job interviews for computer-tech jobs out of his unconscious desire to pursue a more Total Self-congruent vocation and lifestyle.

Goddrick discovered through life mapping how his ELDER LEADER part-of-Self was in dynamic conflict with his inner ARTIST. For his *Responsibility* Life Theme, which he associated with an ELDER LEADER Archeme, he felt it was important to hold a standard sort of full-time job in order to be a "good parent."

In the process of marrying, and raising three boys, Goddrick had largely abandoned his artistic passions for the sake of being a responsible breadwinner. When he had been single and through his early years of marriage, Goddrick was active in the music world along with his wife, an actress and singer herself. He had played saxophone in a band and managed soundstages for several bands who were touring.

When Goddrick envisioned a series of Alternate Future Lifescapes to explore what he really wanted to do for a job, his gut impulse—that is, his inner ARTIST's vision—was that he desired to teach saxophone in his garage, so he could get back to playing and sharing his passion for music.

Soon after completing his life-mapping sessions, Goddrick found an ad one day inviting local community members to join a band. He retrieved his sax from a closet and he not only joined the main band but he also started playing in a smaller ensemble that plays regularly at local community venues. These were not paying gigs, but when he went to another tech job interview shortly after joining the band, he was hired on the spot. He attributed this success to being more relaxed at the interview due to feeling more fulfilled from returning to his music.

Since then, Goddrick continued to gain and lose a series of tech jobs—as these jobs still were not in synchrony with his inner values and priorities—until starting around two years later, several transformational breakthroughs occurred. First, Goddrick took on a position as a regular, grade-school substitute music teacher. Second, he took a summer job serving as a soundstage manager, in fantasy character garb, at a regional Renaissance festival alongside his wife, who had become a strolling singer there as well. In addition, Goddrick took a seasonal job as a department store Santa Claus, which has since developed into a full-time role as Santa at a North Pole theme park.

His new, full-time job as Santa combines Goddrick's parental ELDER LEADER values with quite his ARTIST's flair! He continues to play sax with the community band, while one of his sons has also come to major in music, specializing in sax, at college.

Goddrick is living out all of his Life Mission core values. He finds his current career and his avocational ventures to be deeply rewarding. He is enacting his Life Mission day by day, dynamically expressing his musical passions, and fulfilling his fatherly responsibilities, all the while realizing his Life Dream.

Your Life Dream

Projecting Alternate Future Lifescapes (*Tool #VI:4*) and identifying your Total Self System goals (*Tools #VI:5* and/or *#VI:6*) has allowed you to prospect a future life course that aligns with your Life Mission.

You are ready now in your life-mapping odyssey to stake a claim—to declare your Life Dream. You may wish to review, reflect upon, and journal about your Alternate Future Lifescapes, your Archeme and/or Life Theme Goals, your Life Purpose statement, your Total Self System goals, and/or your Life Mission Statement to mine these essential yearnings.

You might wish to envision one or more additional Alternate Future Lifescapes that embed or combine what you have already identified as your core values and highest priorities. Or if you prefer, you can focus mainly on the specific Future Lifescape scenario from *Tool #VI:4* that offers the greatest combination of your values and goals, and modify that one further.

Re-envision or compose a best Future Lifescape scenario until it rings true for you as a fulfilling future projection. You may continue to use your Archetype Dialogue Journal along with *Tool #VI:8* to envision and formulate your most ideal Future Lifescape as, indeed, your Life Dream.

Here are some principles to consider as you envision and frame your Life Dream Statement:

- ALLOW FLEXIBILITY (Incorporate core value-based goals rather than fixed material objectives, so that many different outcomes could serve to fulfill your Dream);
- BE WILLING TO RE-ENVISION, YET HOLD TO YOUR CENTER;
- BELIEVE! HAVE FAITH IN YOUR UNIQUE LIFE MISSION;
- ACCEPT AND COMMIT TO EXPRESSING YOUR UNIQUE GIFTS!

> Complete *Tool #VI:8* before continuing.
> (Compose a clear statement of your Life Dream.)

I like to say to each of my beloved pets and to my family and close friends that there has never been before nor will there ever be again in the entire history of creation any other Being (cat, dog, or person!) that embodies all of their specific, wonderful qualities. This awareness pertains directly to your Life Dream Statement, as Martha Graham also expressed beautifully in her affirmation for all of us from *The Life and Work of Martha Graham* (Random House, 1991):

> There is a vitality, a life force, an energy, a quickening that is translated through you into action, and because there is only one of you in all of time, this expression is unique.

I have had Martha Graham's affirmation about the importance for each of us to fulfill our specific Life Mission posted on my office wall for many years, since a therapist once gave it to me on a placard as a gift. Sharing it here brings me full circle to the dream message that launched my quest to develop and deliver this book for you to utilize in the pursuit of *Living Your Dream, Now!*

> **YOU HAVE THE RESPONSIBILITY**
> **TO REALIZE YOUR DREAMS,**
> **NOT JUST FOR GETTING BY.**

Remember:

With your completion of this chapter's *Tools*, you have accomplished Stage II of your life-mapping rites-of-passage odyssey. Your Life Dream Statement is a gem you may carry forward with you across a final Threshold of adventure: to realize your Life Mission by completing your Epic Journey as one true to your inherent nature, values, and joy. You are well on your way to realizing the capacity to *Live Your Dream, Now*!

What remains is for you to "incorporate," with Stage III (chapters 7–9), all of the insights you have gained through your engagement in the first two Stages of your life-mapping journey into your everyday life from here forth. The *Tools* in chapters 7–9 will guide you through the final stage of your Quest.

The completion of this stage of Incorporation (or, Reintegration) is essential for you to undertake so you can effectively apply the treasures you have already obtained. The *Tools* in chapters 7–9 equip you with activities you can use to "ground" your Life Dream and to incorporate your core values and your thematic Archeme Strengths into the fabric of your everyday life.

Chapter 6 TOOLS

Your Life Path Portfolio

VI:1 My Uplifting and Self-Limiting Life Theme Trends
Journal: Which of your recurring Life Themes are the most positive and helpful to you? Which of your Life Themes tend to hold you back or have been sources of frustration, and why, especially in relation to life goals you wish to pursue?

VI:2 My Archetype Dialogue Practice, Step Four: Individual Archeme Goal Statements
Situate yourself in a comfortable, quiet space. Close your eyes and sink into an active contemplation session. Engage with your Archemes in your active imagination and/or conduct a live journaling conversation with your Archemes. Invite each of your Archemes to express their individual goals. Write out each of your Archemes' goals during or after you emerge from your active imagination session.

VI:3 My Life Themes Exploration, Step 4
Journal: Write about your personal goals with regard to each of your Life Themes from your Life Themes Map (*Tool #II:6*).

VI:4 My Alternate Future Lifescapes
Journal: Using first person (I, me) and as if in the present tense, envision and write about two or more possible future scenarios. It is important to write two or several of these scenarios, to cover an expansive array of options. Be as specific and descriptive as you can. Include elements within each of your alternate future lifescape scenarios that describe HOW you have "arrived" at this future set of conditions. Include sample dates for each of your "future casting" scenarios.

(**Example:** [July 4, 2019]—I am living in the Finger Lakes with my family of pets, nearer to my sisters and some life-long friends. It is exciting during the summer months of lake resort activities, and it is less populous but still dynamic and peaceful during the winter. I am finishing the sequel to Your Life Path, called Better Endings.)

VI:5 My Archetype Dialogue Practice, Step Five: Uniting My Archeme Allies Council around a shared Life Mission Goal

Situate yourself in a comfortable, quiet space. Close your eyes and sink into an active contemplation session. Converse with your Archemes in active imagination and/or by live journaling to discover a common goal that your Archemes can all agree to as a positive, shared Life Goal within your Total Self System. Ask your Archemes to help you frame this common goal around aspects of your Life Mission. Invite your Archemes to form an Archeme Allies Council that you can call upon from this point forward in your life, to help you to realize together your shared Mission.

VI:6 My Life Themes Exploration, Step 5: Integrating My Life Themes with a Central Goal

Journal: Write about a core, central goal you have. This should be a goal that positive actions involving each of your Life Themes (from *Tool #II:6*) could help you to bring about. Consider how this one overarching, personal goal pertains to your Life Mission. How can your attitudes or behavior pertaining to each of your recurring Life Themes contribute to fulfilling your primary Mission?

VI:7 My Archetype Dialogue Practice, Step Six: Gathering Archeme Ally Mission Contracts

Situate yourself in a comfortable, quiet space. Close your eyes and sink into an active contemplation session. Invite each of your Archemes to state what specific strengths or attributes s/he can pledge to contribute to help realize your collective Mission within your Total Self System. Ask each Archeme to agree to a contract to commit to their specific contributions to your Mission Goal. Write out these Mission Contract commitments for each of your Archemes, as members of your Archeme Allies Council.

If you have been exploring your Life Themes instead of engaging with the Archetype Dialogue Practice, at this stage you can state your own affirmations for each of your Life Themes regarding how you will focus in each of your Life Theme situational roles to manifest your Mission.

VI:8 My Life Dream Statement
Consider deeply and proclaim a clear statement of your Life Dream. Write this statement in BOLD letters in your Life Path Maps Portfolio Journal or into the bold outlined box provided with your Portfolio Toolkit for *Tool #VI:8*.

This is the Life Dream that you will focus on throughout Stage III (chapters 7–9) of your "finishing" process with this book's *Tools*.

Chapter 7

LIFE IS . . . A BOWL OF CHERRIES: REMODEL YOUR LIFE PATH

Congratulations! You have completed your central Transformation stage of your life-mapping rites-of-passage journey, and you have claimed your Life Dream. This chapter, along with the final two chapters, will conduct you through Stage III, by which you will be equipped to incorporate the awareness you have gained back into your everyday life from your more highly integrated perspective, focused on the attainment of your Life Dream! It is time to bring Home the fruits you have gathered so far along your journey.

The remaining *Tools* allow you to apply the insights you have attained already so you can manifest your deepest potentials. Of course, nothing worth achieving comes without meaningful effort. Your Life Dream will benefit from an operational plan—tasks and concrete actions you can take that will help you materialize your Vision; then you will be fully equipped to *Live Your Dream, Now!*

I can honestly report that most of the individuals I have worked with who have completed a full life-mapping process have since made significant strides toward fully realizing their Life Dream. In addition to the stories I have already shared in earlier chapters, there was Lilith, for example, who came to realize through life mapping how a "part of her"—her ARTIST, IDEALIST, and Shadow-LOVER Archemes, combined—felt that her marriage to a man she had "settled for" was interfering with her pursuit of a life of artistic passion that she had begun in college but largely abandoned after she married. Lilith investigated divorce procedures following her life mapping reflections, until she realized that what she really wanted was to be able to express her artistic talent without allowing any relationship to hold her back. Lilith has since gone forward with her art and photography while also maintaining her family, regarding a more conscious integration of her family responsibilities with her artistic talents as part and parcel of her revised Life Dream.

Some of you have discovered through your life-mapping insights what it is that brings vitality to your everyday activities and choices. Others of you have come to recognize the dynamic roots of your long-standing conflicts or inhibitions, which you had not understood before. For all of you, an ongoing Archetype Dialogue Practice or continuing Life Themes Explorations (see chapter 9) can allow you to check in on your unconscious nudges and impulses as they crop up instead of reacting blindly to triggering situations.

I believe the successful life transformations you can achieve through life mapping are a testament to the resilient, adaptive nature of the human spirit that naturally seeks to transcend conditions interfering with your positive life fulfillment. With a well-integrated human psyche, you have the capacity to more deeply comprehend your life conditions and to harness your Strengths so you can actualize your potentials. It mainly requires your sincere reflection and some conscious planning or redirection to advance past stumbling blocks that may have previously held you back due to your unconscious fears or archetypal Shadow motivations.

Whatever you come to understand, and however you might choose to shift your life conditions in response to your engagement with this book's life-mapping *Tools*, your life course cannot help but to remodel itself as you are rerouting your cognitive outlook. The procedures of life review, life reflection, and future life prospection (which I like to call "future casting") can help you to reorient your mental, emotional, physical, and spiritual outlooks so you can proceed with greater awareness and clarity toward living your optimal life.

But, which comes first? Is it the integration of your Archeme personas via reassembling your role-based identity perspectives, or a shifting of life conditions? I have observed both sorts of life-mapping results. For some people, their Life Story Map reveals that a Sea Change (or a dramatic change in thematic patterns) has already occurred.

Recall Dana, for instance, whose story of hardship and liberation from a harsh foster family I discussed in chapter 2. Dana's Life Path radically transformed when she reached eighteen and freed herself from her prison-like foster home. From a series of (-5) Shaping Events throughout her fosterage years, to almost entirely (+5) events thereafter, Dana made a conscious leap into a new, much more positive life trajectory. It is interesting that after she left the foster home, she joined two religious traditions: Buddhism, which she discovered when she moved initially to Indonesia; followed later by Science of Mind, when she moved back to Colorado. Her spiritual practices with these religions along with their liberation-oriented belief systems helped Dana to reframe and, I would say, to cognitively remodel her Life Path.

People who engage in programs designed to help them intentionally modify their behavior or outlooks, such as Alcoholics Anonymous, psychotherapy, or a religious conversion process, generally can achieve significant changes in Life Theme trends reflected in their Life Maps from before and after becoming involved with such a program.

Other case stories include Raj, Ambrosia, and Joanna, three life mappers who experienced life-changing visionary events that significantly altered their understanding of life and led them to redirect their Life Paths significantly from that point forward. Their stories indicate a common effect. Adopting a positive, programmatic change of outlook on life, whether by relocating to change your everyday environment or in response to a specific nighttime dream or other visionary experience, can lead you to change your life conditions significantly, due to a major insight that influences a reframing of your overall outlook on life!

The anthropologist Anthony Wallace coined a useful phrase to describe how a change in mental outlook can bring about fundamental changes in life conditions, or *vice versa*. He called this a "mazeway resynthesis" (1956, "Mazeway resynthesis: A biocultural theory of religious inspiration," *Transactions of the New York Academy of Science*, Series II, 18 (2), 1956d: 626–38). An entire system of cultural beliefs and values that frame how people in a social group conceptualize their reality can shift—as Wallace's historical examples show—when a charismatic individual ushers in a new vision to help people deal with rapid social change or hardships. Hiawatha of the Iroquois, for instance, communicated about a vision he experienced that led to the formation of the League of the Iroquois, after a devastating period of blood feuding and epidemic disease had nearly decimated the Iroquois nations. Hiawatha's prophetic vision called for major political and ideological changes that set the Iroquois onto a new, more positive path forward—one that empowered them to forge a better, more adaptive, and more peaceful future for many generations to come. Their resulting democratic council system was the model Benjamin Franklin used for the US Articles of Confederation, to frame the very foundations of American democracy.

For individuals, a cognitive mind-set shift or "mazeway resynthesis" can affect how you comprehend and conceptually reframe your entire outlook on life based on your consciously chosen values. Alcoholic Anonymous catch phrases such as One Day at a Time or Easy Does It, for instance, facilitate the sorts of changes in attitude a person can use to remodel their outlook on life. Any sincere, conscious formation of a new set of core values can change your mind-set, which can effectively redirect your future Life Path forever.

Your engagement with this book's *Tools* has empowered you to frame core values and to orient your Life Dream around your personal Mission from this time forward.

I have witnessed many life mappers who have indeed undergone a major shift in their overall outlook on life, allowing them to redirect their life course to manifest their Life Dream.

Hope, for example, is a woman who came to a better understanding of how challenging romantic relationship issues have stemmed from her dysfunctional, early family-related Life Themes of *Abuse*, *Family Drama,* and resulting *Meltdown* events. After completing her life-mapping process, Hope is able to draw upon positive character Strengths she associates with HEALER, COMMUNICATOR, and MYSTIC Archemes. She has sustained a marriage now for several years based on honest, open communication.

Hope's more aware, Archeme-integrated Self was sorely tested when she and her husband lost their home, their dog, and most of their possessions to a ravaging wildfire in Colorado. This time, though, Hope self-consciously entered into a Descent phase and allowed herself a gradual, emotionally honest re-emergence—rather than a debilitating *Meltdown*—to consolidate her energies and come to terms with her losses. She has learned to regularly check in with and listen to the needs and inner urgings of her Archeme Allies, rather than trying to "muster along" without drawing upon these internal Strengths.

Understanding how Life Theme patterns and Archeme perspectives have affected you over time can help you wend your way with greater awareness from where you have come, to where you are now, to a set of life conditions where you realize and maintain your Life Dream. Life mapping is a toolkit you can continue to work with throughout your life. It reveals your role identities and character qualities you have already developed and equips you to illuminate your internal conflicts so you can clear roadblocks and embark on promising new directions throughout your life's continuing adventure.

Use life mapping to envision new pathways and to construct meaningful transitions as stepping-stones from your current point of origin to your desired destinations for positive outcomes. This is like having the blueprint of a labyrinth or a maze before you enter; you can choose which pathway to take to reach the Center and then re-emerge to apply and share your insights from the awareness you have gained.

This chapter's *Tools* guide you to envision a values-oriented Future Life Path and to forge a practical plan of action to manifest your Life Dream. "Out with the old, in with the new" can be your credo from this point forward as you construct a clear pathway to manifest and *Live Your Dream, Now!*

Your Fantasy Future Life Map

A first step toward charting a course to realize your Life Dream, *Tool #VII:1* invites you to explore parameters of your Life Dream by composing a Fantasy Future Mindmap. Your future mindmap is a freely designed drawing, or it could be a collage of images. It represents, through any medium, the sorts of milestone life experiences and needed transitions that are likely to unfold in the process of attaining your Life Dream. It is important for you to approach this early stage of "future casting" in a fantasy-envisioning mode. Be as unrealistic, as romantic, and as idealistic as you wish in projecting a pathway to realize your Life Dream. You needn't concern yourself with practicalities or limitations of any kind at this phase.

Unleash your imagination! Draw or compose collage images to create your Fantasy Future Mindmap freeform. Create several alternate future mindmaps, if you like, until you arrive at a Fantasy Future Life Map that expresses your wildest Dream come true!

> Complete *Tool #VII:1* before continuing.
> (Compose your Fantasy Future Mindmap.)

Explore Your Life Dream

What does your Fantasy Future Mindmap reveal about you and about your Life Dream? What core values have you represented within your map? Do you project yourself as someone like Mother Teresa or Albert Schweitzer, working selflessly to bring peace and solace to the masses? Or, are you gladly sipping Mai Tais while enjoying a gentle ocean breeze on your Maui lanai?

Examine your Fantasy Future Mindmap to identify what personal values it represents. *Tool #VII:2* guides you through a process to identify and list your Core Values related to your Life Dream.

> Complete *Tool #VII:2* before continuing. (List your Core Values
> that are evident from your Fantasy Future Mindmap.)

Make sure your Life Dream is big enough to fulfill your deepest personal values so you can express your highest ideals. This is your chance, right now, to take stock of what you intend to center your Future Life Path around. This is your opportunity to set into motion a future pathway by which you will transcend any current sense of personal limitations.

You have claimed a Life Dream that is yours alone, though you might wish to share it with others. (Be careful, though, not to dissipate the energy of your Dream by sharing about it too openly before you begin the process of manifesting.) If, after creating your Fantasy Future Mindmap and exploring the core values associated with your Life Dream statement (*Tool #VI:8*), you wish to modify or expand your Life Dream statement further, do so in your journal or in your *Portfolio Toolkit* for *Tool #VI:8*.

You may also wish to compose a revised Fantasy Future Mindmap to represent your modified or expanded Life Dream.

Envision Guideposts along Your Pathway to Realize Your Dream

When I have composed a Fantasy Future Mindmap for myself, it usually takes the form of a pathway with move-segments much like the winding course on the Milton Bradley game board of *Life*. There are twists and turns, obstacles and bridges, and every major change in direction represents a significant Turning Point I can anticipate along the way to achieving my Dream. I place relative dates alongside this winding pathway to project my progress with incremental goals according to meaningful though flexible time frames.

Likewise, now that you have established a Fantasy Future Mindmap that can lead you to fulfill your Life Dream, it can be helpful to consider more carefully the sorts of Turning Points or the sequence of specific transitions you can expect to encounter as you proceed toward realizing your goals.

Tool #VII:3 provides a process to help you anticipate possible future transitions and then spotlight each of these, one transition at a time, to envision and contemplate more deeply.

How will you bring about or negotiate each of your anticipated, pivotal turns in the road along your pathway to *Live Your Dream, Now*? How can you prepare for a later transition by making effective adjustments now, or in the foreseeable future? It is important to imagine your future transitions as positive milestones rather than as stumbling blocks or daunting obstacles. As you have already envisioned a complete—though fantasy-based, for now—pathway to realize your Life Dream, each transition, however difficult, will bring you closer to the actualization and fulfillment of your Quest.

> Complete *Tool #VII:3* before continuing. (Anticipate future transitions along your pathway to manifest your Life Dream.)

A Life Dream Focusing Tool

To help you convert your "fantasy" future mindmap to a realistic, self-actualizing Future Life Map, *Tool #VII:4* invites you to engage in a Life Dream Focusing technique. To assist you in exploring your Life Dream, place your Life Dream statement or a word, phrase, or image representing your Life Dream in the center of the page and then to explore four sets of considerations that relate to accomplishing your Life Dream: Outcomes, Obstacles, Resources, and Solutions. Simply make note of any ideas that come to mind for you in relation to each of these four quadrant areas on the chart. You can use bullet-point statements or even images if you prefer to represent your considerations with respect to each of these four aspects.

The Life Dream Focusing Tool is a brainstorming technique. You might begin by expressing the positive results you anticipate from realizing your Life Dream in the Outcomes quadrant of the chart. Then, zoom in upon potential challenges or limiting conditions that could affect your pursuit of your Dream. At the same time, you can use the other two quadrant spaces on your chart to identify resources and potential solutions by which you could resolve these challenges.

The Life Dream Focusing Tool could help you to develop practical steps and strategies you can employ to realize your Dream. It may help you anticipate some additional transitions or to refine your Fantasy Future Mindmap (*Tool #VII:1*), so you can incorporate available resources and plan proactively to implement solutions to possible obstacles you might otherwise confront along your path.

If you wish, compose several different Life Dream Focusing pages, to explore either your Life Dream as a whole or any specific subgoal or issue pertaining to your capacity to realize your Dream. When you focus active attention on your goals and consciously, as well as unconsciously—via tuning in with Archeme Dialogue journaling—troubleshoot your issues in advance, this can help you to strengthen your resolve to manifest your Life Dream. The Life Dream Focusing Tool can also help you expand your awareness of your Dream's most beneficial potential outcomes.

> Complete *Tool #VII:4* before continuing. Explore some future challenges and solutions with the Life Dream Focusing activity.)

Meet Your Future Self in the Mirror

Another future prospecting activity, *Tool #VII:5*, lets you stake your claim and plant your intention more deeply to *Live Your Dream, Now!* Simply stand before a mirror and imagine or enact a conversation with your Future Self. Imagine the reflection in your mirror is you, either after you have fulfilled some intermediate goal or after you have fully integrated your Life Dream into your everyday life. For more fun with this, try wearing a piece of clothing, visible in the mirror, that represents for you your Dream achieved.

Ask your Future Self, as if from a "parallel world" overlapping with this one, about her or his life. Especially ask what steps s/he has taken to achieve the Life Dream you are now seeking to realize. Record your imaginary dialogue after you have finished at the mirror, or sit before the mirror with your journal or *Toolkit* pages open and write your conversation out as it occurs.

Let me try my own pen at this briefly for you, as an example:

LW: *So where are you living, Linda?*

MIRROR *I travel between two homes and around the world!*

(Future Linda): *I own a house near a lake in New York and a winter rental cottage in Ireland. I live most of the year, when not traveling for life-mapping workshops and seminars, in my lakeside home, just an hour or so from my sister. Sometimes another sister or some friends join me here to vacation or to conduct their own retreats. I have a rental cottage on my property, too, which I rent out for people coming for life-mapping workshops and classes. I co-own the cottage in Ireland, which I visit for writing retreats and to conduct workshops for a few weeks every year.*

LW: *That sounds nice!*

MIRROR: *It is.*

LW: *But, Linda, how can you afford two homes in retirement?*

MIRROR: *Look into how best to manage and further build your retirement income. Remember to envision clearly, and trust in your own process.*

LW: *This feels like a time traveler's paradox . . .*

MIRROR: *It's a Loop; you have contacted me in my Now. You are to me but a visitation in memory from my former Self! Things are clearer in retrospect, of course. But you CAN get Here, or else this conversation wouldn't be happening in the first place!*

Complete *Tool #VII:5* before continuing.
(Dialogue with your Future Self in the Mirror.)

Have fun with your Meet Your Future Self in the Mirror active imagination Tool! Maybe you could call it, "Who's the Fairest?" I recommend for you to engage with your Future Self in the Mirror several times, especially as you contemplate or approach a specific transition along the course you have established to manifest your Life Dream. Keep transcripts of your Future Self conversations after you finish your process with this book; you could copy and further extend these conversations in a dedicated section of your Archetype Dialogue Journal.

A Time Capsule Treasure Chest from Your Future Selves — Forging Your Pathway Forward, One Step at a Time

Following in a similar vein yet with a more process-oriented approach from your conversations in the mirror with your Future Self, *Tool #VII:6* allows you to step down your Fantasy Future Mindmap to build a practical, self-actualizing plan of action.

"A Time Capsule Treasure Chest from Your Future Selves" (*Tool #VII:6*) offers a Message-in-a-Bottle sort of journaling process.

Imagine that, as you proceed forth to *Live Your Dream, Now*— living according to your Core Values and gradually manifesting around yourself the full expression of your Life Dream—you keep a running log of significant, milestone sorts of achievements along the way. With each entry, you describe where you are from having attained that level of achievement in the process of fully realizing your Life Dream. As well, imagine that after making each log entry to mark a significant achievement, you roll it up like a scroll of parchment, tie a colored ribbon around it, and place it in a wooden box, like a Treasure Chest some adventuresome Pirate might fill with gold.

Now then, imagine further forward that when you reach that moment along your future Life Path when you wake up one day and realize you are Now fully Living Your Dream daily, you place a final entry log scroll into your Treasure Chest. A time-space portal opens on your bedroom's computerized wall that morning (future technology is truly amazing!). You lovingly place your Treasure Chest, filled with all of your time capsule scrolls, into the portal, which whooshes it back in time to appear in a future journaling activity of your Present Self, the very journaling session you are engaging with *Tool #VII:6*.

Discover this time capsule Treasure Chest or box. It is not locked. Open it up and you will discover the neatly wrapped event logs placed there with so much thoughtfulness and love for You by your future Selves—that is, by You at various stages of your progression to *Live Your Dream, Now!*

Open the scrolls in the Treasure Chest, one at a time (after you have written these for *Tool #VII:6*), and read through them several times. Number the entries to arrange these log events in the order by which you believe your Future Selves would have deposited them (they are not dated). This ordering helps you reconstruct sequential time frames.

As you organize the significant future possibilities your Time Capsule Treasure Chest entries represent, you are composing a Plan of Action to realize your Life Dream. Refer to this Life Dream Action Plan as you create an Actionable Future Life Map at the end of this chapter's répertoire of *Tools (Tool #VII:8)*.

The Time Capsule Treasure Chest journaling process lets you creatively envision a realistic, flexible Action Plan by which to manifest your Life Dream. The very practice of envisioning incremental steps and anticipating gradual transitions to fulfill your unique Mission imaginatively forges a clear pathway you can use to ground your intention and buttress your commitment to *Live Your Dream, Now!*

Because you can imagine your Dream fulfilled, you can live it; in your imagination you are already Here! All it takes Now is for you to nurture your intentions and actualize your goals by implementing the sorts of goal-fulfilling actions you have already envisioned!

> Complete *Tool #VII:6* before continuing. (Compose log entries for your Time Capsule Treasure Chest from Your Future Selves; Arrange these logs to construct your Life Dream Action Plan.)

Accentuate the Positive!

Next, I invite you to add further substance to your Life Dream Action Plan. *Tool #VII:7* provides a finishing process that integrates your Life Theme and/or Archeme Strengths into your practical plan of action for realizing your Dream. This *Tool* guides you to arrive at "one thing" you can incorporate into your life that will propel you on a direct course to *Live Your Dream, Now!*

Do you remember the character Curly from *City Slickers I*? Shortly before he expires, Curly aims to share his wisdom with Mitch about the "secret of life"—to uncover the "one thing" that everyone needs to achieve their life's fulfillment:

In *City Slickers II*, Mitch learns from Curly's twin brother Duke that the "one thing" varies with every person; it is that which will allow him or her to be true to themselves. For Duke, it is "honesty and integrity," which he adheres to at the end of the story by sharing with Mitch and their fellow adventurers the treasure chest of gold they have sought.

"Accentuate the Positive!" is a Tool that equips you to put into action that "one thing" that is true to your own Core Values and Mission and that will irreversibly launch you in a positive direction to *Live Your Dream, Now!*

As with the rest of these life-mapping *Tools*, I have piloted "Accentuate the Positive!" with myself and many other people to develop it as an effective technique. After identifying Life Themes and Archeme Strengths as well as some Shadow qualities I felt I could draw upon to manifest my own Life Dream nearly a decade ago, I arrived at a rather sudden "eureka" realization of "one thing" I could do that would actively propel me to accomplish my Dream, and then I did it! My archetypal psychology therapist at the time was the one who encouraged this action.

Despite not having adequate savings to permit me to easily take such a leap, I left my home to a house sitter and rented a chalet for a full month's writing retreat in Steamboat Springs, Colorado. I brought with me only Ariel, my elderly, beloved harlequin calico cat. I worked eight to twelve hours per day nearly every day for that whole month, developing a book proposal and assembling an initial outline and a full set of preliminary chapter drafts for what has eventually become this book. Many of the self-discovery *Tools* you are using here emerged during that retreat; I have never stopped developing and sharing these life-mapping procedures and *Tools* from that time forward.

Later steps opened up for me following that first bold step of taking a one-month writing retreat. I attended three writing workshops over the next five years, each of them serving as a significant stepping-stone, propelled by the momentum of that original act. At the third writing conference, I met the agent who has helped me to publish this book. So, that initial "one thing" of the writing retreat set into motion for me a long-term process that achieved a remarkable outcome.

I encourage you to use *Accentuate the Positive!* to discover your ONE THING (*Tool#VII:7, Step F*) that will propel you into motion along a direct trajectory to realize your Mission and fulfill your Life Dream. Then, of course, DO THAT! Make sure your ONE THING is a significant departure from your day-to-day life that will irreversibly launch your Life Path in the direction of realizing your Life Dream.

Your ONE THING will require more than a lifestyle change like simply going on a diet or adding a morning walk every day. Acting on your ONE THING can be the most important step in your life-mapping adventure, for it empowers you to truly Cross a Threshold to actualize your Dream.

> Complete *Tool #VII:7* before continuing.
> (Complete the six-step Accentuate the Positive! technique.)

Bring It Home: Your Self-Actuating Future Life Map

Once you have completed this chapter's *Tools VII:1–7*, you are ready to design your Self-Actuating Future Life Map (*Tool #VII:8*). Proceeding further from your Alternate Future Lifescapes (*Tool #VI:4*) and your Fantasy Future Life Map (*Tool #VII:1*), your Self-Actuating Future Life Map provides you with a practical road map with realistic marker events to serve as milestone or guidepost transitions. This "finishing" Map visually represents your pragmatic Action Plan for manifesting and *Living Your Dream, Now!*

It is important for you to plan the incremental steps and pivotal Turning Points in your Self-Actuating Future Life Map around the sorts of Core Values you wish to realize in your future (e.g., happiness, harmonious relations, or making a fulfilling contribution), rather than around attaining specific material objectives like a particular job, location, or relationship. A values-oriented approach allows you to actualize your Dream while remaining flexible and open to various opportunities.

For example, instead of positing on your Map that you will work at a particular job in a specific city within a predetermined time-frame, you can project eventually working at a job or mastering a hobby that allows you to express your creative talents in a naturally beautiful location that inspires you daily. See the difference?

The life-mapping and journaling activities that you have engaged in with this book's *Tools* shall remain in your alchemical chemistry kit, as it were—that is, in your personal development repertoire of helpful strategies and techniques—forever. You can re-apply any of these *Tools* and modify or remodel your plans as you continue to actualize your personal values and Live Your Dream, even as your vision of your Life Dream continues to shift and unfold further over time.

It could be useful for you to model your Future Life Dream Action Plan (*Tool #VII:8*) in the form either of a labyrinth or a spiral that proceeds, step-by-step, or arc by winding arc, gradually into a Center that represents arriving at the core of your Dream's greatest potentials. Designing your plan as a circular labyrinth or as an ascending spiral rather than as a linear (left-to-right) flowchart schematically frames your Life Path as a heartful and flexible, holistic adventure instead of a linear and possibly self-limiting sequence of dutiful tasks.

Consider, for example, the design of the sacred Rose labyrinth at the Chartres Cathedral, represented below:

Notice how the Rose labyrinth's pathway unfolds gradually, traversing interlinked quadrant segments and building like Maurice Ravel's musical crescendo in his *Bolero* to a more integrative awareness as the labyrinth walker slowly unwinds their thoughts and feelings in meditative silence. Allow your Future Life Dream Action Plan to incorporate a balanced progression of phases that will integrate your Core Values (see your reflections for *Tool #VII:2*) and your unique Strengths (e.g., from your Archemes or Life Theme role-traits). Let your Self-Actuating Future Life Map unwind a gradual process by which you will achieve your Life Mission and actualize your Dream.

Your Life Dream Future Action Plan is not a fifty-yard dash to the dutiful completion of self-ordained tasks; it is rather like walking a labyrinth as just described. Or, perhaps it might be for you like walking along a winding, serene country road with gradual twists and turns, some helpful road signs, sunshine dripping through verdant (or, snow–covered!) trees along the way, and with footbridges arching across murmuring creeks. However you might personally choose to represent the path of your unfolding experience as you set out to *Live Your Dream, Now!,* may it infuse your life with meaningful values that issue from and ultimately return you to the Center of your Heart.

Complete *Tool #VII:8* before continuing.
(Compose your Self-Actuating Future Life Map.)

Chapter 8 provides an important finishing step to round out your life-mapping rites-of-passage journey. Chapter 8 *Tools* equip you to ground and to re-integrate the insights you have gleaned for the purpose of Living Your Dream.

Chapter 7 TOOLS

Your Life Path Portfolio

VII:1 My Fantasy Future Mindmap

Mapping: Compose a Fantasy Future Mindmap. It might resemble a game board with a winding pathway or use any image format you choose. Create your map in your Portfolio Journal or on a separate piece of paper. You can then reduce (shrink) a copy and place it into your journal; or use the page provided in your *Portfolio Toolkit* for *Tool #VII:1*.

VII:2 Core Values of My Life Dream

Journal: Reflect upon and write about the Core Values or ethical ideals that you associate with Living Your Dream.

VII:3 Future transitions *en route* to Living My Dream

Make a descriptive list of significant transition points or life changes you can bring about or that you expect to encounter as you proceed forward to realize your Life Dream.

VII:4 My Life Dream Focusing Activity

Write your Life Dream Statement (from *Tool #VI:8*), or place an image to represent your Life Dream achieved, in the center of a page designed according to the sample template shown below. You can use bullet-point statements or images to brainstorm ideas that pertain to the four quadrant dimensions of Outcomes, Obstacles, Resources, and Solutions. Begin with Outcomes, to establish a perspective of envisioning "from the end achieved."

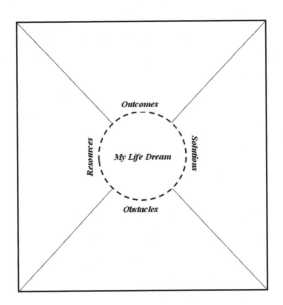

VII:5 Conversation with My Future Self in the Mirror

Journal: Have a dialogue with your Future Self. (You may copy the image below and enlarge it to use and then paste it into your Portfolio Journal, or use the image provided in your *Portfolio Toolkit* for *Tool #VII:5.*)

VII:6, *Step A* **My Future Time Capsule Treasure Chest**
Imagine reaching several transition-points in your future where you realize you are proceeding in a positive direction to achieve your Life Dream. Make a brief log for each of these significant events or summarize them briefly in a series of scrolls such as represented below. You may copy the scroll image below multiple times and paste these copies into your Portfolio Journal, or use the set of scroll templates included in your *Portfolio Toolkit* for *Tool #VII:6, Step A.*

Number each log consecutively in the white rectangle on each chest as you envision and compose them, but do not date them. Your envisioned future events do not need to be in chronological order, and they may or may not pertain directly to your Life Dream goals. (Save your final log, in which you will record having achieved your Life Dream, for Step B below.)

VII:6, *Step B* **My Future Time Capsule Treasure Chest**
My Life Dream Achieved! Write one more treasure chest event log from your point of view of an envisioned future moment when you realize you have fully realized your Life Dream. Write using first person (I, me) and in the present tense. Describe your life at this stage with as much descriptive detail as you can. Express how you are Now (in your envisioned future) living in accord with your Core Values. Be sure to include your future viewpoint about how you have arrived at this Self-Actualized condition.

VII:6, *Step C* **My Future Time Capsule Treasure Chest**
Imagine next that you open this treasure chest from your future in your current time and you take the scrolls out to read them. (The treasure chest is not locked.) Review the set of scroll logs you have

composed, and reorder them according to what seems to be a likely chronology for these events to occur so that they reconstruct the pathway you "will have taken" to realize your Life Dream. List this ordering of logs in your Portfolio Journal or in the final scroll template included in your Portfolio Toolkit for Tool #*VII:6, Step C.*

VII:6, *Step D* My Future Time Capsule Treasure Chest
My Life Dream Action Plan Add relative time frames to your reordered, chronological list of your Treasure Chest Event Logs from Step C (as illustrated below). Compose this as your Life Dream Action Plan for realizing your Life Dream.

Example:

Time Frame	*Event*
(April 2017)	(Completed full set of life-mapping webinar series)
(August 2018)	(Relocated to NY State)

VII:7, *Step A* Accentuate the Positive!
Journal: State clearly a Major Goal related to your Life Dream. Write about this Goal, describing why it is a major priority for you to achieve.

VII:7, *Step B* Accentuate the Positive!
Make a list of all of your Life Themes from your Life Themes Map (*Tool #II:6*) and of your Archemes that you have associated with these Life Themes on your Archemes Map (*Tool #III:5*). Next to each Life Theme and/or Archeme (as illustrated below), make a complete list of some positive (Strength) and/or negative (Shadow) character qualities that you identify with each of your Life Themes and Archemes.

Example: *Family* Theme / ELDER LEADER Archeme / Positive qualities: Support, Stability / Negative qualities: post-traumatic stress, self-confidence issues.

#)	Life Theme	ARCHEME	Character QUALITIES	
			Positive	Negative
	_____	_____	_____	_____

VII:7, *Step C* Accentuate the Positive!

CIRCLE from among your STEP B entries all of those Character Qualities—whether positive (Strength) or negative (Shadow) traits—which you have associated with your Life Themes and/or your Archemes that could be helpful to you in realizing your Life Dream Goal identified in Part A. List just those circled qualities in a separate list that you could represent in circles as illustrated below in your Portfolio Journal or in your *Portfolio Toolkit* for *Tool #VII:7, Step C.*

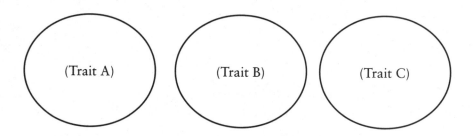

VII:7, *Step D* Accentuate the Positive!

Journal: Referring to the Life Theme and/or Archeme qualities you have identified for Step C above, brainstorm about *HOW YOU CAN APPLY THIS COMBINED SET OF QUALITIES* to realize your Life Dream Goal.

VII:7, *Step E* Accentuate the Positive!

List or journal about specific, concrete ACTIONS you can take to bring about the ideas you have stated for Step D, still based on Qualities you have identified from Step C.

VII:7, *Step F* Accentuate the Positive!
Journal: Identify and journal about ONE THING, based on the Actions you have identified from Step E, that you can commit to integrate into your life in your foreseeable future. Let this ONE THING be an action or new behaviors that will irreversibly LAUNCH you in the direction of realizing your Life Dream.
Include: When will you do this ONE THING?

VII:8 My Self-Actualizing Future Life Map
Mapping: Design a Future Life Map image to represent your process for manifesting your Life Dream. (You may wish to use a large sketch pad or a poster board page. Then reduce/shrink a photocopy to paste into your Portfolio Journal; or use the page provided in your *Portfolio Toolkit* for *Tool # VII:8.*)

Chapter 8

LIFE IS . . . A MOUNTAIN WITH VISTAS: GROUND YOUR DREAM

You have identified and staked a claim on your Life Dream. You have an Action Plan, with maps at hand, and you have set a practical course to manifest your Dream. It is time for you to gradually "live into" your Dream, to manifest and *Live Your Dream, Now*! Your work with this chapter's *Tools* will supply you with creative tokens to ground your progress. These *Tools* can help you stay the course once you have finished your life-mapping adventure with this book.

The third stage of your life-mapping rites-of-passage process calls for you to incorporate the insights and lessons you have acquired along this journey back into your everyday life. You are ready to "bring Home," in mythic terms, the products of your illumination, so that you may benefit not only yourself but your entire world by living according to your Core Values and sharing from the wisdom you have gained.

By *Living Your Dream, Now!* you serve life from the core of your integrated, uniquely individuated Self. That is what is at stake as you step forth and manifest your Life Dream. No one else can live and serve from the potentials of YOUR Dream, but You!

In *The Wizard of Oz* during the final stage of this Epic-Comic Adventure, Dorothy and her Archeme Allies dissolve the Witch of the West's Shadow-ELDER LEADER energy. Dorothy assimilates the power of the Wicked Witch by taking the broomstick from her dissolving form. Then Dorothy's Archeme Allies return together to the MYSTIC Wizard's castle at Emerald City, where he bestows upon them tokens to symbolize their growth and achievements. These tokens acknowledge the Strengths that each of Dorothy's Archeme Allies has developed by succeeding with their individual challenges and by working together harmoniously through their collectively shared ordeals.

The character qualities that each member of Dorothy's ensemble cast has sought to develop—mature Awareness (Dorothy), Wisdom (Scarecrow), Heart (Tin Man), Courage (Cowardly Lion), and Responsible Independence (Toto)—have been within them all along. Glinda tells Dorothy she "has had the power all along," because Dorothy wears the ruby slippers she magically acquired when her house fell on the Wicked Witch of the East.

Now the Wizard, though he is not truly "All Wise and Powerful," is at least rather resourceful and a good judge of character. He knows what his charges have needed all along, which are primarily two things.

First, they needed the experience of drawing upon their inherent Strengths to gain awareness and to develop their own as well as their ensemble capabilities. Second, following their successful Quest, they will benefit from receiving Totems—a diploma for the Cowardly Lion, a heart watch for Tin Man, and a diploma for Scarecrow—to help them remember their Strengths as they carry forth from their accomplishments into the future.

Likewise, you stand poised at the returning embankment of your second mythic Threshold, from which position you are equipped to Live Your Dream day by day from this time forward. You, too, have grown from identifying and reintegrating archetypal Ally Strengths and/or Life Theme role traits that have been within you all along. Your engagement with the challenging tasks of honest life review and deepening reflection have revealed to you your hopes and dreams, your key challenges, and your recurring stumbling blocks. Your Archeme and/or Life Theme related character traits aligned within your Total Self System embody qualities you can draw upon forevermore as you consciously *Live Your Dream, Now!*

To ground your Dream and carry forward with your Life Dream Action Plan, you too can benefit from assembling Totems as you step forth daily to enact and fulfill your Mission. A heroic adventurer carries with them a Totem or symbolic tokens of their personal Strengths, in the form of a weapon, herald, talisman, shield, and/or special clothing or insignia of honor.

I love the portrayal in the image below of Saint Joan of Arc, one of my personal favorite WARRIOR/MYSTIC figures. Joan's armor represents the fortitude of her character. She wields a sword to symbolize her patriotic loyalty and justice that prevails due to her courage and selfless service. Notice also in this iconic image of Saint Joan the column of white light that descends from the heavens to encircle her head. This indi-

cates to me her divine connection along with the higher awareness she humbly relied upon to fulfill her mission to protect a people. St. Joan drew deeply from her Archeme WARRIOR and MYSTIC Strengths to fulfill her spiritual calling.

I acted in a play while in college called *Chamber Music* (Arthur Kopit, 1962) wherein I portrayed a schizophrenic woman in a mental ward who believed she was Joan of Arc. I wore a metallic fencing jacket and mask—ironically, I was on my college fencing team at the time—and I dragged along with me wherever I went this huge, awkward, plywood cross. My second line in the play was about this cross that I had difficulty pulling through a door frame while making my entrance as Joan. "It came with the armor!" I proclaimed about the burdensome cross. And so it did, as a Totem of St. Joan's religious grounding.

Totemic representation is a method you can use to embody symbolically your core values and ideals. Totems express our identities and "contain" our potentials. Someone might carry a rabbit's foot, for example, to physically represent the positive potentials of "luck." A baseball pitcher might wear such a talisman around their neck, or maybe a special pair of old socks, as a constant reminder of the inner Strengths they possess that result from their disciplined practice and talent. What we might call "luck" in this sense is actually not random; it is the product of the person's concentrated, disciplined focus on a goal or ideal which they have developed the intrinsic capacity to achieve. A Totem is a symbol that can help you magnify and focus your energy in the process of achieving your goal.

This chapter's *Tools* provide tried-and-true methods to symbolically ground your Life Dream. This is an essential finishing phase. Totemic grounding will empower you to resume your everyday life equipped with a lasting awareness of the Strengths you have developed and the actions you have committed to implement from this time forward.

The Totems you may assemble with this chapter's creative activity *Tools* can assist you to carry your values and intentions forward as you advance to *Live Your Dream, Now!* Each of the Totems you will create is significant. Together, these Totems are "take-aways" from your self-discovery adventure with this book, like a diploma of graduation or an insignia of initiation. Your life-mapping Totems are to remind you of your Archeme and Life Theme Strengths, of your Core Values and Mission, and of the Life Dream you have set your sails to manifest for the benefit of all.

Your Life-Mapping Totems

For the remainder of this chapter I will provide a background for each of the Totems you can create with the chapter-final *Tools*. You will infuse these Totems with the inherent Strengths of your powerful, heroic Self. They can help you in the future to stay true to the course you have established to fulfill your Mission and to manifest your Life Dream.

Your Animal Totem Talisman

What kind of animal are you? What animal qualities could represent your Archeme Ally—or, your multiple role identity—character

Strengths? Your Animal Totem or set of Totems can harness your power of intention, like a magnifying lens focuses the heat potential of the Sun.

Tool #VIII:1 leads you to discover and represent your personal Animal Totem(s) that will accompany you like a Native American animal spirit guide along on your heroic daily Quest. Animal appearances in your recurring dreams or animal associations with any of your Archeme Allies represent archetypal Anima/Animus qualities that you may claim as Strengths.

Do you choose the Animal Totem, or does the Totem choose you? I acknowledge a Tiger as one of my lifelong animal Totems because of a long series of recurring Tiger dreams I described in chapter 4. My image of this Animus figure (usually a masculine power form) has transformed over time as I have unfolded along on my own life path to better assimilate and integrate this energy.

My early Tiger dream image was a fearful apparition—a frightfully powerful male Animus friend that turns fierce and chases after me. Over time I have come to own this energy so that my later Tiger dream images have shifted to being playful, friendly cubs I can hold in my hands. Archetypally, Tiger has come to represent for me a constellation of ELDER LEADER, MYSTIC, and WARRIOR traits that I feel grateful to contain and carry forward.

Do you identify with a favorite animal figure that appears in your recurring nightly dreams or is in some way symbolically meaningful for you? Why? What Strength or Shadow qualities does this archetypal animal figure represent about you? Perhaps you have more than one animal Totem. Use *Tool #VIII:1* to represent as many as you choose!

Complete *Tool #VIII:1* before continuing. (Compose artwork or obtain a material object like a stuffed animal or other token of your Animal Totem or Totems.)

Your Living My Dream *Collage*

The credo for the life-mapping process you are implementing with this book's *Tools* is *Live Your Dream, Now!* This means you do not have to wait for some nebulous future conditions to occur in your life in order for you to step into the life of your Dreams, fulfilling your Purpose and serving your Life Mission, Now! This is because you have framed your Life Dream in terms of Core Values and Strengths you have already developed in your mythic Life Story rather than by merely material, pie in the sky objectives.

You are already in the initial stages of Living Your Dream. You have defined your Life Mission and reclaimed your inherent Strengths so you can better fulfill your reason for being here, day by day! You have remodeled your vision of your future and you have set a practical yet visionary course for manifesting your Life Dream from this point forward.

Tool #VIII:2 invites you to create a manifestation collage to represent how you are already living with an eye to fulfilling your Dream, as well as how you are gradually "living into" the full conditions of your Life Dream. I call this totem your *Living My Dream* collage. It is designed like an archery target with images composed within three concentric bands that illustrate, from the outer ring to the Center: what you are doing Now; what you anticipate as foreseeable future transitions; and your Life Dream itself, fully realized.

Your *Living My Dream* collage is yours to remind you of the Action Plan you have designed that will serve you in manifesting your Life Dream.

I encourage you to play with or to adapt this *Living My Dream* collage to suit your current use and, of course, you are free to repeat or to modify your collage as you might wish. You may find it valuable to compose various "target" image collages as you anticipate new transitions in connection with some newly emerging or shifting vision of your Life Dream.

I recommend for you to place your completed *Living My Dream* collage in a highly visible or significant personal space, such as on your office wall or in your bedroom or on a bathroom mirror. You could even transfer your collage images onto a fabric. Contemporary photographic transfer methods allow you to place your collage onto a blanket, linen, or comforter fabric that you can order online.

Reflect on the images in your *Living My Dream* collage for inspiration as you celebrate your gradual process of realizing your Dream. Chapter 9 *Tools* will equip you with some additional ways to reinforce your progress and to maintain your commitment to realizing your unique Mission and Dream.

> Complete *Tool #VIII:2* before continuing.
> (Create your Living My Dream Collage.)

Your Archeme Allies/ Life Theme Strengths Mandala

I hope you will go forth after completing your life-mapping adventure with this book's *Tools* ever more aware of the Strengths you derive from your Archeme Allies that you have developed in relation with your dominant Life Themes. Your situational Archeme/ Life Theme-related traits are not fragmented, random, or necessarily buried shards of hidden unconscious impulses, as persona Archetype characteristics are often portrayed in the popular press. Whenever you begin to feel conflicted inwardly or you have a decision to make involving a dynamic set of options, take the matter at hand to your active imagination practice or directly to your Archetype Dialogue Journal. There you can openly explore your unconscious motivations, fears, or desires.

Invite your Archeme Allies to speak up and to speak out as they wish. Their happiness and sense of fulfillment are vital to your success in living your life according to your Total Self System's integrative values and goals.

The Archemes you have identified and that you have encountered with your Archetype Dialogue Practice are associated with situational roles and social identities you have developed and enacted throughout your life. It is appropriate to recognize the character quality Strengths that these thematic-archetypal "ensemble cast" members embody within your psyche. *Tool #VIII:3* invites you to create an Archeme Allies/ Life Themes Strengths Mandala that celebrates the holistic Strengths you have developed that assist you to *Live Your Dream, Now!*

Carl Jung defined a mandala as an artistic representation of the "archetypal state of the Self." You can create a mandala to represent dynamic interrelationships among elements that characterize the psyche or your Total Self System at a specific time or for a particular context. Your Archeme Allies or Life Themes Strengths Mandala depicts qualities of your unconscious or situational identities that you can draw upon in a balanced way as you proceed forward with all your endeavors.

To design your Archeme Allies/ Life Themes Strengths Mandala for *Tool #VIII:3*, center your composition around an image that represents for you the successful realization of your Life Dream. Around that central image of your Dream achieved, you may arrange magazine or online images, your own artistic representations and/or words and phrases that illustrate your Archeme/ Life Theme Strengths that contribute to the fulfillment of your Dream.

The sample Archeme Allies/ Life Themes Strengths Mandala shown below is my own. Around central images representing my Life Dream achieved, I have arranged online clip art images that represent Strengths I associate with five of my Archeme Allies: IDEALIST, COMMUNICATOR, WARRIOR, MYSTIC, and TEACHER. I have also included images celebrating two of my recurring dream *animus/ anima* figures of Tiger and Bear.

The Archeme Allies/ Life Themes Strengths Mandala is a holistic Totem that lets you ground and center your intentions. It is like a magnifying lens that focuses your Total Self System on the fulfillment of your Life Dream from a unified perspective. As with all of the totemic devices provided with this chapter's *Tools,* you may create additional mandalas to center your attention upon Alternate

Future Lifescapes or to explore a transitional phase toward Living Your Dream.

> Complete *Tool #VIII:3* before continuing.
> (Create Your Archeme Allies and/or your Life Themes Strengths Mandala.)

A New Vista: Your Life Metaphor from the Vantage Point of *Living Your Dream, Now!*

Congratulations, Life Mapper! You have already begun to *Live Your Dream, Now!* The attention you have given to engaging with your life-mapping *Tools*, including your creation of Totems for this chapter, have remodeled your Life Path from this point forth, forever.

You have envisioned desired destinations and charted practical pathways to arrive there. You have set into motion clear intentions in relation to your Core Values and your Mission Statement that harmoniously resonate with your Life Themes and integrate the goals of your primary cast of Archeme Allies within your Total Self System. You have discovered and reclaimed your greatest Strengths and you have developed methods to attend to and resolve internal conflicts in a manner that you can incorporate seamlessly into your life.

There is no going back from this new vista you have achieved. You are now more consciously aware of who you are, where you are going, how you will get Here, and what you can contribute from fulfilling your unique Life Mission. This is a very meaningful, growth-bestowing achievement.

You are like Dorothy and her ensemble cast—or, if you prefer, the protagonist you identified with your Parallel Myth technique (*Tool #III:9*)—each Archeme character now better realized in Strength, going forward together through "thick or thin." Remember the insight about how Toto must survive after Dorothy has grown to own her own power as a mature, integrated Self? You, too, will naturally continue forward from Here to live out your Life Dream, because you can!

As your Life Story has shifted direction to allow you to embrace and express your Life Dream that will become more and more fully manifest day-to-day from this time forward, your internal perceptions about Life itself are also naturally changing. The pairs of statements shown below are Life Metaphor statements that some life mappers have expressed at the beginning (before they undertook a Life Path mapping process), and then again after they had completed this rites-of-passage journey:

Life Is . . .

BEFORE:	AFTER:
a path in a deep forest with multiple paths	a winding road, with many paths but only one is right
a puzzle	a perfect painting/ balanced in color and shape
a giant maze with turns and twists	a glow pop: hard and bittersweet, then soft and sweet
a path with multiple paths	a fairy tale: struggles but with a chance for a happy ending
a forked path in a forest; no map	climbing a mountain, but the peak is not windy but calm
a jigsaw puzzle without a picture on box	an adventure with no permanent mistakes
Colorado weather	a summer that never ends/ happiness
a lottery ticket/ random luck	a lightning bolt at night; you can briefly see your path
three paths at a crossroad	still a road, but with road stops along the way
a game of poker	winning a triathlon: accomplishment/ fulfillment

Notice how the "Before" Life Metaphors included above reflect a good deal of uncertainty and trepidation about these peoples' futures. The dramatic shift revealed in these same persons' "After" Life Metaphor images demonstrates the transformational capacity of Life Path mapping as a valuable method for resolving uncertainties and for highlighting positive potentials for personal growth and development.

To conclude this chapter with a story, meet Mercedes, a fifty-four-year-old woman who engaged in an intensive, six-month life-mapping program aiming to determine how best to proceed with her life and career. Mercedes offered the following Life Metaphor when she began her life-mapping sessions: "Life is like a duck in water; it appears calm on the surface, but its feet are thrashing wildly underneath." Mercedes's Life Themes Map is shown below in the form of an Excel stacked area chart; this Excel format tracks the prominence of her Life Themes over time.

Mercedes's Map shown below clearly reflects her *Duck-in-the-Water* metaphor. Notice particularly the high number of negative-impact Shaping Events that Mercedes charted below the neutral Age line from her Life Themes Map:

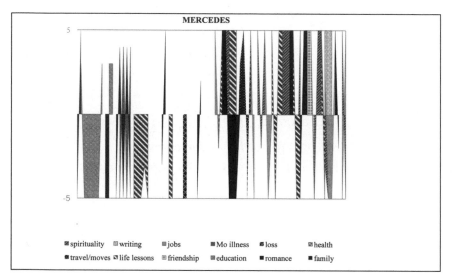

Life Themes Key

Through her life-mapping reflections, Mercedes arrived at a deeper understanding of the Life Theme she called *Life Lessons*, which she associated with a TEACHER Archeme. She came to recognize the many Strengths she has developed through surviving difficult challenges. After reaching this realization, Mercedes designed a Future Life Map and an Action Plan to fulfill her Life Dream of becoming an author and teacher.

When I asked Mercedes to express a current Life Metaphor after she had fully completed her life-mapping process, this time she replied: "Life is like a Gentle Breeze blowing continually over the Ocean, bringing blessings, Wave after Wave!" Isn't it fascinating how Mercedes's same Life Themes Map shown above can convey both of her two diametrically different Life Metaphors?

With this more positive *Ocean Blessings* Life Metaphor grounding a more positive outlook on her life overall, Mercedes has since moved forward with great strides toward fulfilling and living her Life Dream. She has relocated closer to family in a stable environment, and she is making a living through writing and teaching while further progressing with her spiritual life.

Imagine you are NOW fully Living your Life Dream. What is your Life Metaphor from this new vantage point of having fully realized your Mission, your Dream? What, to you from the perspective of your Life Dream fulfilled, is a human lifetime like, and how?

Complete *Tools #VIII:4–5* before continuing. (Envision your Life Metaphor from the vantage point of *Living My Dream, Now!* Then, repeat the Life Path Satisfaction Scale self-quiz.)

Chapter 8 TOOLS

Your Life Path Portfolio

VIII:1 My Animal Totem Talisman
What Animal image represents your greatest Strengths of character? Is there an Animal figure from recurring dreams that you recognize as an Anima (feminine) or Animus (masculine) energy? Journal about the Strengths this Animal Archetype energy represents as an Archetype Ally assisting you to realize and maintain your Life Dream. Place images of your Animal Totem in your Journal or *Portfolio Toolkit* to represent your Strengths. Find a stuffed animal or other token of your animal to keep with you or place it in a meaningful place that you see daily.

VIII:2 My *Living My Dream!* Collage
On a poster board or sketch pad, draw a large circle with two smaller concentric circles to resemble an archery target. Use the outer circle space to represent activities you can be practicing in your life Now that are aimed toward gradually bringing about conditions to manifest your Life Dream. Let the second, middle band represent future

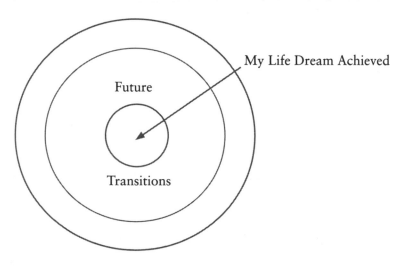

transitions or milestone sorts of events that will propel you closer to fully living your Dream. The center circle represents you fully living your Dream in a foreseeable future scenario. Write some of your Core Values, Life Theme qualities, Archeme Strengths, and intermediate Goals onto these spaces first in pencil, then find magazine pictures or online images (or your own artwork) representing these, to paste onto your collage.

My *Living My Dream!* Collage

VIII:3 My Archeme Allies or Life Themes Strengths Mandala
Place one or more images that represent the fulfilled realization of your Life Dream in the center of a separate poster board or on a sketch pad. Around that central image, compose a Mandala by drawing in or pasting images that represent your Archeme Strengths and/or the Strength Qualities you have developed through enacting your Life Theme role identities that, together, can assist you to actualize your Life Dream. Paste a color copy of your Mandala into your Portfolio Journal or in the space provided in your *Portfolio Toolkit.*

VIII:4 My Life Metaphor from *Living My Dream, Now!*
From the vantage point of fully Living Your Dream, what, to you, is a human lifetime like? Compose or paste an image to represent your New Life Metaphor of what your life is like, from the vista of your Life Dream fulfilled.

VIII:5 The Life Path Satisfaction Scale (self-quiz, #2)
Rate your degree of agreement to each question on a separate page (or in your Life Path Maps Portfolio for this Tool), according to a 1–5 scale, using the following rating scale:

(1: Not at All; 2: Somewhat; 3: Neutral; 4: Usually; 5: Always)

1. I am confident in my ability to realize my dreams.
2. I have access to all the guidance I need in order to succeed.

3. I have a strong sense of my own life's purpose.
4. I am satisfied with major life decisions I have made.
5. I know where I want to be/ what I want to be doing in the foreseeable future.
6. I generally set clear goals in my life and then strive to achieve them.
7. I have realized most of my life goals.
8. My dreams have been a valuable source of inspiration for me.
9. I have a clear sense of direction in my life now.
10. I know what my next step is and how to take it.

LPS Index Score (add your scores for 1–10, then divide by 10).

COMPARE this score with your previous LPS Score from *Tool #I:8*. **What is your <u>degree of change</u> in this index score (plus or minus)?**

Chapter 9

LIFE IS . . . BETTER ENDINGS: LIVE YOUR DREAM, NOW!

I have for several years nurtured a fun idea that I will present more fully in a sequel to this book. The book opens with playful narrative retellings of just the endings of some novels and popular movie scripts that, to my sensibilities, end less well than I would personally wish as they were originally written or filmed. You know the feeling of walking out of a theater or putting a book down after turning the final page, wishing the ending might have turned out differently. Then if you read or see the story a second time, you might vainly hope that this time it might end differently. Maybe—like me—you've even fantasized about what could have happened to the characters at the end instead, in some parallel universe where story endings turn out better, or at least more in accordance with your liking!

Wishing for a "better ending" to a story is like waking from a bad dream or from a dream you were enjoying until it was rudely interrupted by some external event. You might close your eyes to go back into the dream (in a daydream situation). You could also imagine altering the ending of the dream or to complete it, resolving it in a way you would prefer. This is actually a helpful technique for working with your dreams; and, just as you can imaginatively revise your nighttime dreams, you can likewise envision how you might change conditions in your day to day world, to forge a better ending.

I first arrived at this idea of Better Endings while watching the Peter Jackson movie version of *King Kong*. Knowing all too well that the tragic demise of Kong was imminent, I left the theater while Kong was yet alive, clenching his beloved Ann Darrow (Naomi

Watts) in one hand while teetering atop the needle of the Empire State Building. The military loomed large on the scene already and everyone in the audience knew what was about to befall, all too literally: the Great Kong. I just did not have it in me this time around to stay and watch—or, to agree to—the fateful Fall of Kong or of the magnificent, gigantic forces of Nature that he represents, toppled by the cold machinations of the insensitive, all-too inhumane world. Instead, I left the theater and went to a coffee shop, put pen to notepad, and re-scripted the ending of the King Kong parable much more to my liking. In my "better ending" version of the tale, of course, Kong lives!

Kong's fateful fall from the Empire State Building still happens in my retelling of the tale. But this time, with Ann still in one hand, Kong breaks his fall twice on the way down out of sheer willpower, snatching desperately at the side of the building and thus slowing his descent out of a super-primate adrenaline rush, fueled by his love for Ann Darrow and an unwillingness to let her die. At the base of the building where Kong lands with his beloved, he is injured by the impact but he has survived. Still out of a passionate effort to protect his beloved Ann from the dark forces of urban inhumaneness, Kong gets up while the military has stalled from closing in (presuming Kong could not have survived such a fall). Kong limps, with the unconscious Ann still in his hand, back to the frozen lake in Central Park where she and he had communed in the film version just before their trip up the Empire State Building.

Ann revives after they have reached Central Park. She leads Kong deep into a trailless, woodsy region she knows as a personal refuge in the Park. There they lie low while Ann uses a powerful backstage walkie-talkie that for protective reasons the screenwriter Jack Driscoll had put into her pocket (in 1933 there are no cell phones). Ann calls Jack—still in my version played by Adrien Brody—who is also smitten with her. Given this chance to win Ann's heart, Jack surreptitiously arranges to rent a large truck with a canvas cover. He waits for the dirigible searchlights to depart, then he drives to where Ann and Kong lie hiding, Kong by this point nearly spent by his exertions. Kong scrapes himself forward to follow Ann up into the covered truck bed. Jack and Ann cart Kong off to—have you guessed?—a recently constructed Primate Center in New Jersey. The sympathetic director of the Center, Jane (of course!), immediately takes to Kong and gives him sanctuary.

To summarize from the conclusion of my revisionist story: The renamed Giant Primate Center constructs an entire wing for Kong, bringing in flora and some of the least harmful fauna from Kong's native island to the sanctuary. Ann's acting career soars; she marries Jack and eventually they have three kids who grow up ecologically aware and primate-friendly. Ann visits Kong every weekend at the Primate Center. Jane teaches Kong sign language so he can communicate, a skill for which Kong shows a remarkable aptitude as he represents the missing link paleoanthropologists have been seeking for over a century. Kong lives to contribute to greater human compassion and increased awareness about the innate intelligence and loving, spiritual capacity of our Gigantus-primate cousins.

> Complete *Tools #IX:1–2* before continuing.
> (Make a list of some popular stories that you wish would have alternate endings. Choose one of these and compose your own "better ending.")

I can clearly envision the jacket cover for this re-visioning book: a title, *Bitter Endings*, with an omission line struck through the letter *i,* an insertion caret, and the letter *e* placed on the raised line above. So, the title reads: "*Bitter*; (but no, scratch that . . .): *BEtter Endings*"!

The principle of Better Endings is relevant to concluding your life-mapping odyssey with this book, as it is the underlying premise of your commitment to *Live Your Dream, Now!* This book's *Tools* have equipped you to script a better ending for your own future Life Path as you step forth to manifest the fullest potentials of your Life Dream.

Yet please, I encourage you to remain realistic and flexible. Now that you have crafted an Action Plan to realize your Dream, living It to manifest its greatest potentials will require your attentive, steadfast nurturing and pruning. Would you spread grass seed and expect it to grow without watering your new lawn thoroughly until the first young shoots appear and then regularly ever after?

A lifetime is like an artist's portfolio; it is always a work in progress. As a final debarking stage, as you will soon close this book and steer off to build and enact your excellent, remodeled future, this chapter's *Tools* provide a portable life-mapping toolkit to help you stay the course while remaining flexible through the fulfillment of your Dream and beyond. Equipped with the Totems you have created with chapter 8 *Tools*, this final chapter's *Tools* equip you to check in periodically while you advance to fulfill your personal Mission.

Staying the Course

The following activities complete this book's self-discovery toolkit. I provide these final *Tools* for you to carry forward as adaptive, continuing practices. I encourage you to integrate them into your life on an ongoing basis, as you step forth daily to *Live Your Dream, Now!*

Live Your Dream, Now! Guidepost Log

Guideposts are meaningful transition points or road markers that help you take stock of your progress while you proceed toward realizing your goals. The *Live Your Dream, Now!* Guidepost Log (*Tool #IX:3*) provides a journaling activity for you to use to Check In at incremental steps for up to five years from when you finish your process with this book's *Tools*. This journaling activity mirrors the Time Capsule Treasure Chest future-to-present logging (*Tool #VII:6*) from your present Now until you have achieved and are fully Living Your Dream.

Your Archeme Allies Journal

Your Archetype Dialogue Journal from here forth can become your Archeme Allies Journal. Your situational Life Themes/Archetype character modalities that you have identified since chapter 4 are members of your primary ensemble cast of Allies forever, like Dorothy's special friends from *The Wizard of Oz*. You can check in with your Archeme Allies—individually or by addressing them collectively as your Archeme Allies Council—by descending into an active imagination, Archetype dialogue session whenever you wish. Your Archemes may call out for you to listen to their helpful promptings, too, and they may show up in your dreams, along your journey ahead. Checking in with your Archeme Allies can serve as a tune-up when needed, helping you keep your various Life Theme role orientations aligned and your Total Self System as a whole in harmony with your overall progress and sense of well-being.

From now on, whenever you are feeling doubtful or conflicted about a decision or about any situation that arises, remember you can include your Archeme Allies in your considerations. For a deeply conflictual situation, use the Dynamic Archetype Dialogue, Step Three of the Archetype Dialogue Practice (*Tool #V:10*), to present the matter to two or more of your opposing Archeme perspectives. This can help you to arrive at a better understanding of your internal conflict, and to develop a more balanced approach to your situation that all of your parts of Self can weigh in on and accept.

Everybody has Archeme parts-of-Self that they have naturally developed in relation to their dominant Life Themes. You have identified and forged a connection with these too often submerged points of view and feeling orientations through your Archetype Dialogue Practice or Life Themes Explorations. To maintain these connections, it will be helpful for you to check in with and communicate with your Archeme sub-selves, and review your thematic role perspectives. Other archetypal sub-selves may also show up as you continue with Archeme Dialogue journaling into the future.

Allow your Archeme Allies to express themselves from within your Total Self System. While you continue to grow personally in pursuit of fulfilling your Life Mission and Living Your Dream over time, your ever-evolving internal diversity will also continue to grow and develop.

Your Life Dream Journal

You might wish to combine several of these chapter 9 journaling *Tools* within one journal volume, creating separate compartments for the various modes of checking in and regular journaling you will maintain from this point forward; or you might prefer to maintain separate journal volumes for each of these modes. Your Life Dream Journal can combine in itself both your regular dream journal for recording and reflecting upon your nightly dreams, and your ongoing daily journal that helps you keep track of your insights, ideas, and experiences as you live forth into fulfilling the Life Dream you have committed to realize from this time forward. Your Life Dream Journal can be as mundane or as creative as you are feeling from day to day, but I invite you to think of it as your Life Dream manifesting log. Journaling from this intention can help you keep your Core Values, your Life Mission, and your ever-evolving focus on *Living Your Dream, Now!* at least lightly on your mind, always.

One helpful dream interpretation technique, from *The Art of Spiritual Dreaming* by Harold Klemp (Eckankar, 1991), is to establish a Dream Dictionary at the back of your nightly dream journal. In your Dream Dictionary, when a significant and/or recurring dream image occurs, record that image in your Dream Dictionary. Include the date of your dream and describe the context and your current interpretation of the dream image in detail. You will find that over time, your recurring dream images will change in their form and meaning, in ways that reflect either your own positive growth with regard to relevant situations, or negative feelings of reversal or stagnation in your life.

As I shared in chapter 4, Tiger and Bear images have been some of my own recurring dream images, reflecting aspects of my own unconscious dynamics. Being chased by these Animal forms in my dreams revealed to me a tendency to project my *animus/ anima* powers onto others from a fear of becoming overly aggressive myself. As I have come to balance and to better "own my own power" over time, these Animal dream images have dramatically transformed. My Dream Dictionary helps me to reflect on these internal changes.

Keeping a Dream Dictionary can help you monitor and check in with your progress while you continue to integrate your conscious and unconscious perspectives and motivations over time.

Recurring dream images may directly represent your Archeme Allies. Dreaming and paying attention to especially your more vivid or lucid, self-aware dreams is a natural psychological mechanism for integrating and maintaining interaction with your personal Archeme energies in all their dynamic complexity, significantly "on their own turf."

Active imagination and your Archeme Allies Journal can help you keep in touch with your ensemble cast of Archeme Allies. Likewise, your nightly dreams and unprompted visions are indispensable windows into the deeper recesses of your unique, personal unconscious dynamism. The more attention you give to your dreams overall and the more you attend to your archetypal motivations, the more accessible—and, flexible—your self-actualizing Life Dream can become!

A Life Path Mapping Tools *"Patch-kit"*

The final "bag of tricks" provided for you with this chapter's *Tools* includes a package of life-mapping *Tools* that you can rely on as a portable patch-kit. You should expect that your Life Dream is likely to shift and flex—as it must, to remain vital!—while you continue to develop and express your unique sense of purpose and mission. The Life Path Mapping Tools Patch-kit contains a select combination of this book's *Tools* that you can apply whenever you desire to re-envision your future Life Path or to stay on course with expressing your Core Values and fulfilling your personal Mission.

Living Your Dream is a dynamic process that will shift and adjust as you move ahead with your continuing, fresh opportunities and challenges. That is why it is so important to frame and, as necessary, to occasionally reframe your Life Dream in terms of your Core Values and Mission, which themselves may also morph or assume new significance for you over time.

Your Life Dream is not about obtaining a specific material object, nor is it about acquiring or holding onto a specific job, relationship, or activity. If your Dream is focused too narrowly upon such material ambitions, then as soon as you might fail at achieving or maintaining one of these goals, your whole Dream might appear to shatter, see? *Living Your Dream, Now!* is about ensuring a high quality of life that you can establish and maintain, allowing your current values and your shifting goals along with a flexible, balanced sense of your personal Mission to guide your choices and actions.

The Life Path Mapping Tools Patch-kit includes the following *Tools* from chapters 7 and 8 that you can apply anew when you face a personal decision or a new opportunity or challenge.

- My Fantasy Future Mindmap (*Tool #VII:1*);
- My Future Time Capsule Treasure Chest (*Tool #VII:6*);
- My Self-Actuating Future Life Map (*Tool #VII:8*); and
- My *Living My Dream* Collage (*Tool #VIII:2*).

This Patch-kit combination of elements equips you to reforge your Alchemical creations as you explore alternative vistas along whatever future life course you ultimately choose to travel. That said, any of the Tool elements throughout this book, as well as the entire three–stage life-mapping rites-of-passage process provided with this book's toolkit, remain forever in your chemistry lab, as it were, from this time forth.

May you advance to your greatest happiness and fulfillment!

Consider *Tools #IX:3 and #IX:4* before continuing. (How to Utilize Your Life Dream Guidepost Log Journal and Checking In with your Archeme Allies Council to check in with your progress toward Living Your Dream, Now!)

Postscript

As a parting thought to you as you are now an accomplished Life Path Mapper, I offer what I have often advised Anthropology students about to embark upon interview-based research studies. I tell them: "Everyone has a story to tell; and almost everybody loves to tell their story."

I suppose that insight, which I learned from my own mentors to pass along, has laid the groundwork for me to develop these life-mapping *Tools*, by which you and those with whom you wish to share this book can indeed Tell Your Story, both to yourself and to others.

I find that the above insight has expanded for me over the course of assembling this book, based on the far-reaching potentials of the art of Life Path Mapping:

Everyone has a Dream to Live;
and almost everybody loves to LIVE THEIR DREAM.

May the Epic-Comic Adventure story I sincerely hope you will live to tell and share with others be no less than Your Life Dream Come True.

Chapter 9 TOOLS

Your Life Path Portfolio

IX:1 My list of stories or movies I wish would end differently
Make a list of stories or films whose endings you wish could be changed.

IX:2 A Better Endings story
Choose one of the stories you have listed for *Tool #IX:1* and compose your own "better endings" story.

IX:3 My Life Dream Guidepost Log Journal
Begin your Log of actions and events that help you to *Live Your Dream, Now!* Enter dates and record significant "guidepost" sorts of events, as illustrated below.

Example:

Date   *Guidepost Activity or Event*

_____   _____

_____

_____   _____

_____

IX:4 Checking In with my Archeme Allies Council via my Archetype Dialogue Journal (or, Reviewing my Life Themes)
Whenever you like or whenever you might be feeling internally conflicted or not fully "of one mind" or you are feeling out of balance or uncertain regarding some significant decision or action, use your Archetype Dialogue Journal (or, start a new one) in order to Check In with the members of your Archeme Allies Council. Ask inwardly,

using active imagination, what any of your Archemes may wish to share or express regarding the decision or action. Write down your dialogue with the Archeme(s) that "speak up." If you have been reflecting on your Life Themes instead of or in addition to engaging with the Archetype Dialogue Practice, to Check In with your Life Themes, simply take time when you approach a significant decision or action to review how this decision or action might affect or contribute to your development regarding each of your recurring Life Themes.

APPENDIX

The Twelve Universal Archetypes, by Debra J. Breazzano, MA, LPC

The following tables expand the characteristics of the Twelve primordial Archetypes adapted from (the late) Dr. Charles and Nin Bebeau and presented in the table in chapter 4 on pages 74 and 92. These Archetypes are " . . . psychological patterns that appear throughout human experience and can be seen in the motifs of age-old myths, legends and fairy tales found in every culture . . . and in the imagery of the dream (Aizenstat, 1987)." They derive their images from the four elemental states of Earth, Air, Fire, and Water combined with the three universal energy phases of Creation, Maintenance, and Dissolution. These twelve distinct energetic patterns have correlations with alchemy where transforming base metal (lead) into precious metal (gold) mirrored what Jung called the individuation process of the human soul seeking wholeness. The core themes of this elemental, alchemical process influence the description of these archetypal profiles that appear throughout human experience and guide our personal and collective psychic development.

Each archetypal pattern contains purpose and meaning in its expression. The primordial energy of the Archetype seeks its own unique objective, satisfying its mission. When the "Archeme" or archetypal character associated with a recurring Life Theme of our personalized life story is acknowledged and supported, there is the benefit of a sense of power and cosmic support. Aligning your consciousness with the myths of the archetypal characters discovered in your unconscious creates a strong sense of connection to divine purpose while navigating life's challenges.

The descriptions in each subcategory of the archetypal tables that follow list the essence and strengths of the Archetype within its positive expression except for the subcategory entitled Shadow characteristics. The Shadow is the negative expression of the archetypal energy that has become blocked or exaggerated and is distorted. All twelve Archetypes exist within our being; however, the degree of blending and expressing the Twelve—and whether positively or in Shadow—is unique to our own life path and is dependent on the makeup of our psychic and perhaps even our genetic blueprint (DNA). Although each primal pattern has a distinct impression that is described, the Archetypes most often do not appear in isolation but in combination with one another, shaping our unique personality. How we experience our soul's mythic journey resonates on the four primary levels of what makes us human: our mind, emotions, physical body, and spirit. What we are interested in, how we behave, and the people we are drawn to all correlate with the unique archetypal profile or "ensemble Archeme cast." Having an understanding of the Twelve Archetypes while you navigate this life path process provides a paradigm and vocabulary for discussion for the benefit of not only ourselves but also others. The archetypal insights into our personalities enables us to understand and respect each other's unique, yet also familiar, expression during our life journey.

Each Archetype also correlates with astrology as recorded in Sumerian origin myths and as developed by serious astrologers over the ages. Metaphorically, the core nature of the Archetype is represented by the theme associated with the planet's life force. This archetypal actor (planet) wears their zodiac costume (sign) and acts out their drama on one of the Twelve stages or astrological Houses. In ancient times, astrology was not the nonsensical horoscope readings of modern times, but an empirical science that had origins in astronomy and thousands of years of studying the cosmos with its parallel events and patterns reflected below. Today, planetary astrology has been replaced with zodiac sign-based astrology for entertainment, dismissing this archetypal correlation as unworthy of deeper understanding. The specific correlation is included on the tables for those who have continued to find meaning through the study of astrology.

There is much more to explain and consider than is presented here in the tables. These tables provide notes for quick reference. Pay attention to the distinct traits described in each of the Twelve archetypal charts. As you reflect on the various traits listed, consider which fit for you especially in relation to your own Life Themes. Some may describe you. Some may not. Notice which characteristics of the Twelve Archetypes would be included in your ideal personality profile. Which aspects do you embrace or reject? Do you recognize any Shadow traits? Which Archetypes tend to dominate and which do not? Read chapter 4 to learn more about the practical application of these concepts, and see chapters 5–8 to engage with the Archetype Dialogue Practice that will allow you to engage with your Archeme cast members in an integrative manner through active imagination and journaling.

The Elder Leader

Archetype of Structure
and Authority

Alchemical Correlation	Astrological Association
Earth originating; coming into being	January Capricorn

Mission/Purpose: To provide structure, leadership, and authority for the benefit of the group or community

Mental Traits

- Logical, linear, rational thinker
- Mentally alert within a structured program; awarded for accomplishments
- Good memory for detail
- Values status quo
- Conservative beliefs; traditionalist

- Mental resiliency; strong work ethic
- Mental discipline: organized, systems thinking
- Wisdom and maturity in thinking, even as a young child

Emotional Expression

- Values composure rather than display of emotions
- Can detach from emotions or emotional expression
- Thinks through emotions; rationalizes

- Focuses on feelings of respect (respecting others, being respected)
- Emotional satisfaction through discipline (with self, with others)
- Values commitment and devotion

Physical Aspects

- Body correlations: bones, spine, teeth, joints, skin
- Correct posture important, reflecting pride and dignity

- Medical problems may include: osteoporosis, arthritis, broken bones, dental and dermatological concerns
- Sex for procreation

Spiritual Tendencies

- Monotheism fits well: Christianity, Judaism, Islam as examples
- Devout with their faith and conservative religious beliefs

- Traditional rituals and spiritual practices are valued

Shadow Characteristics

- Critical and judgmental (of self and others)
- Intolerant of others with differing beliefs
- Brutal with discipline

- Autocratic, dictatorial, and often corrupt leadership
- Rigid; unforgiving

Interests/Involvements

Positions of authority or responsibility: politics, legal systems, military, education, government, business

Personifications

- Religious, Military, Political, and Business Leaders

- "Uncle Sam"
- Wise man; Wise woman

The Artist

Archetype of Creative
Expression

Alchemical Correlation	Astrological Association
Earth maintaining	May Taurus

Mission/Purpose: To beautify the world; to take spirit and give it form

Mental Traits

- Visual Spatial aptitude
- Symbolic mentality
- Processes information slowly as images translate into language
- Once beliefs are decided, resistance to changing or adjusting them
- Simple, yet profound, thought
- Prefer learning by doing rather than learning through school systems
- Strong work ethic and mental discipline when involved with their craft or in support of others

Emotional Expression

- Creative expression of emotions through music, song, dance, writing, poetry, works of art etc.
- Values loyalty
- Can be moody although very dependable
- Passionate about their craft
- Artistic ambiance in surroundings is important for sense of well-being

Physical Aspects

- Body correlations: throat, tongue, lips, chin (cleft often), thyroid
- Medical problems may include: sore/ strep throat, thyroid problems, cleft palate, lip and mouth ailments
- Very sensual
- Sex is sensual expression of the Divine through loving, physical union; enjoys oral sex

Spiritual Tendencies

- Religious traditions that include both gods and goddesses fit well
- Take the essence of God/Spirit and give it form as an act of worship

- Create great works of art and architecture in honor of the deity
- Sacred rituals involving all senses especially song, dance, and divine symbols

Shadow Characteristics

- Can hold a grudge or hold in negativity until explode with rage
- Passive-aggressive
- Stubborn (bullish) in mind-set even when shown to be mistaken

- Resists and/or resents artists/artistic expression
- The flaky artist
- Disdainful of formal education or so-called "intellectuals"

Interests/Involvements

Positions that allow hands-on applications and creative expression: Art (performing, visual, collection of, etc.), musician, architecture, landscaping, farming, carpentry, and construction

Personifications

- Your favorite artist, musician, vocalist, or dancer

- Leonardo Da Vinci, Mozart

The Healer	Alchemical Correlation	Astrological Association
Archetype of Service and Healing		
	Earth dissolving	September Virgo

Mission/Purpose: To provide service through healing of humans, plants, and animals

Mental Traits

- Very smart; yet, appears to be slow mental processor as considers all the details and connects various relationships
- Keeps knowledge organized "exactly" and simply into replicable patterns

- Intuitive thought; gut wisdom as source of knowing
- Perfectionist; can become obsessive with thinking

Emotional Expression

- Sensitive emotions
- Service-oriented; offers emotional healing assistance
- Enjoys intimacy but also requires time alone to balance emotions

- Anxiety can partner with self-doubt
- Emotional satisfaction when involved with nature and animals; can become overstimulated emotionally in densely populated areas

Physical Aspects

- Body correlations: small intestines, left arm and hand, left lung and diaphragm, pancreas, and immune system
- Unrushed, sensitive sex; enjoys making love in nature

- Medical problems may include: having sensitive GI/digestion, vulnerable immune system (AIDs, frequent infections), and respiratory concerns along with problems with left arm/hand

Spiritual Tendencies

- Nature-/Earth-based religions appeal such as shamanism
- Expresses spirituality through rituals, often combining elements for holistic healing through connection to the Creator

- Lives in service to god and/or goddess
- Needs spiritual connection for sense of well-being, more so than other archetypal energies

Shadow Characteristics

- Self-critical; critical of others
- Perfectionism leading to not completing tasks
- Oversensitive and defensive

- Type A; obsessive; extreme anxiety
- Extreme introversion
- Atheist

Interests/Involvements

Positions that allow healing relationships to occur between humans, animals, or with nature: medicine, mental health, veterinary, zoology, science, and math fields for assisting with solving society's problems

Personifications

- Mother Teresa
- Dr. Doolittle

- Shamanistic or naturopathic healer

The Lover

Archetype of Relationship

	Alchemical Correlation	Astrological Association
	Air originating Air creating	October Libra

Mission/Purpose: To create balanced union in partnership with self and others

Mental Traits

- Diplomatic mind-set; good conflict mediation
- Ability to look at all sides, weigh and balance
- Logistically savvy; able to mentally multitask
- Collaborative leadership style
- Symbolic and linear thinker

Emotional Expression

- Feels most settled when involved in healthy, intimate relationship
- Internal union with their "opposite other" is important for well-being
- Commitment to relationship is important
- Flirtatious, charming
- Appreciates beauty and romance
- Values justice
- Cooperative

Physical Aspects

- Medical problems may include: kidney stones, bladder infections, lower back aliments
- Romantic sex for expression of love and union
- Body correlations: kidneys, lower back, waist, bladder
- Physically attractive although prone to love handles

Spiritual Tendencies

- Spiritual and religious practices that embrace ideas of divine union and sacred partnership fit well
- Finds god in the arms of another person
- Divine union as internal union with Self

Shadow Characteristics

- Narcissistic; a "player"; unable to keep commitment to monogamy in their relationship
- Avoids conflict and confrontation
- Indecisive, as sees all sides of issue
- Can give their whole heart in relationship, only to abruptly take it all back and move on
- Possessive, jealous
- Codependent

Interests/Involvements

Positions relating to "balance" and beauty: legal systems, diplomacy, negotiation, counseling, collaborative leadership, social directors, interior designers, beauticians

Personifications

- Romeo and Juliet
- Aphrodite
- Eros

The Idealist

Archetype of the Synthesizer

	Alchemical Correlation	Astrological Association
	Air Maintaining	February Aquarius

Mission/Purpose: To assist humanity in achieving a higher level of consciousness; bring about a resolution of paradoxes for transformation of the collective with insightful ideals

Mental Traits

- Quick mind with brilliant flashes of insight
- Intuitive sense of "I know"; arrives at answer without deductive or logical reasoning
- Visionary; far-reaching mind

- Focus on future rather than past
- Independent thinker
- Will often think and do the unexpected
- Creative, innovative thoughts; seeks freedom from conventional ideas

Emotional Expression

- Not necessary to get "deep" or intense with emotions
- Gets along well with different "cliques"— can adapt to any social group setting—but doesn't feel as if they fit in; often feels as if they're odd person out

- "Happy go lucky" emotional attitude
- Feel compassion and empathy, but not emotionally codependent
- When confronted about behavior or ideas, tend to think process through rather than respond emotionally

Physical Aspects

- Body correlations: circulatory and nervous system; ankles and lower leg
- Appear exotic or nerdy-looking and often dress without a sense of fashion trends
- Bisexuality and attracted to the unusual or taboo

- Medical problems may include: high blood pressure, epilepsy, and seizures, anxiety/nervousness, ankle, and lower leg issues
- "Love the one you're with" attitude regarding sexual encounters

Spiritual Tendencies

- Embrace a wide range of spiritual expressions; eclectic spiritual beliefs

- Can relate to the origin myths that includes alien encounters or supernatural beings

Shadow Characteristics

- Rigid when set on ideals
- Intolerant or impatient of others when they have different ideas
- Dedicated to projects, but not always dedicated to the work ethic that allows projects to be completed; lazy

- Prankster; antagonizer
- Procrastination as they consider many ideas; often hard to get started on project or task
- Love collective idea of humanity, but individuals/humans with their flaws irritate them

Interests/Involvements

A wide range of pursuits professionally relating to social causes that assist humanity; multiple careers, including inventors, program directors, project managers; require autonomy and sense of freedom within their professional position

Personifications

- Einstein or Marie Curie
- The Nerd, The Trickster

The Communicator

Archetype of
Communication and
Connection

Alchemical Correlation	Astrological Association
Air-dissolving	June Gemini

Mission/Purpose: To link; to connect; to be a messenger

Mental Traits

- Synthesizer; able to connect a variety of concepts for greater knowledge
- Strong memory
- Enterprising curiosity; wants to understand "why?"
- Enjoys learning

- A very quick, sharp mind; analytical
- Verbal processor; ability to articulate thoughts well
- Technology-oriented through the programming mentality

Emotional Expression

- Thinks through emotions
- Rationalizes

- Tries to understand emotions; analytical
- Articulates their feelings

Physical Aspects

- Body correlations: right arm, right lung, respiratory, hands, eyes
- Sex that includes words (written or spoken) is a turn on

- Talk with hand gestures; great dexterity
- Medical problems relate to the hands, eyes, right arm, and also include respiratory issues such as bronchitis and ammonia

Spiritual Tendencies

- Connect to the Divine through words (i.e., Scriptures) and prayer

- Religious/spiritual practices that include reading, writing, reflecting fit well

Shadow Characteristics

- Duplicity; can deceive
- Won't speak; stonewalls
- Chatterbox; no off switch
- Pathological liar as they have the ability to keep track of their various deceptions/stories

Interests/Involvements

Positions relating to communication and hands-on dexterity: computer programming, website development, technology, phone solicitors, handyman, editor, author, lecturer

Personifications

- Mercury, the messenger of the gods
- Bill Gates
- Conductor of orchestra with grand hand gestures

The Warrior	Alchemical Correlation	Astrological Association
Archetype of Individuality	Fire-originating Fire-creating	April Aries

Mission/Purpose: To pioneer change; develop personal power

Mental Traits

- Competitive mind; enjoys mental challenge
- Quick thinker; not brilliant but good ideas
- Problem solver; innovative
- Mental resiliency
- Kinesthetic learner
- Independent thinker, but will follow directions of respected leaders

Emotional Expression

- Independent in managing their emotions
- Pride in ability to endure physical challenges and stress
- Can be fiery, assertive
- Confidence with sense of personal power; determination
- Processes emotions through their body
- Passionate in support of their beliefs and causes
- Quick to anger, but also quick to forgive; doesn't hold grudge
- Protector; values loyalty

Physical Aspects

- Body correlations: head, temples, neck, sinus, adrenalin
- Values being in shape, athletic, healthy, toned throughout life
- Sex is very physical; athletic; enjoys "make up" sex
- Very physical with approach to life; enjoys the rush of speed, competition, and challenge
- Medical problems may include: headaches/migraines, hypochondria, stressed adrenal glands

Spiritual Tendencies

- Focus and commitment to the Quest for the proverbial Holy Grail
- Following the Cause becomes Divine
- Crusade oriented, . . . "in the name of God"

Shadow Characteristics

- Verbally tactless; speaks without thinking
- Aggressive; bully
- Physical intimidation; abusive
- Impulsive; selfish
- Whimp, fearful of their power

Interests/Involvements

Positions that have physical aspects and support their cause: recreational and professional sports, marketing and sales, travel adventure, social activism

Personifications

- Your favorite social activist
- The hero/ine
- The knight in shining armor
- Athena

The Golden Child Archetype of Inspiration and Balance	Alchemical Correlation	Astrological Association
	Fire-maintaining	August Leo

Mission/Purpose: To rule from the heart, inspiring others

Mental Traits

- Thinks big picture; logical and visionary
- Goal-oriented when leading the cause; persuasive speaker
- Mentally balanced; integrates multiple perspectives
- Manages mental stress well

Emotional Expression

- Charismatic, charming, inner glow
- Inspirational, remaining sensitive to others
- Responsible, dependable; even tempered
- Childlike playfulness
- Determined to succeed, to rally and empower others
- Kind, benevolent, protective guidance
- Appreciates flattery and compliments and is generous in response
- Can become heartbroken when neglected
- Dramatic; enjoys being center of attention

Physical Aspects

- Body correlations: heart, chest, upper back, spleen
- Enjoys dressing to fit the setting
- Radiant, shining features
- Medical problems may include: cardiovascular issues, heart attacks, murmurs, upper back, and spleen problems
- Sex is playful, sensual, and dramatic

Spiritual Tendencies

- Incredible confidence from birth as if channeling the Divine
- Relates to mono- and polytheistic religions
- Spiritual leadership

Shadow Characteristics

- Cult leader
- Narcissistic, egotistical
- Immature, needy, spoiled
- Arrogant and believes they are the center of the universe

Interests/Involvements

Positions where they can rise to the top of their preferred type of "kingdom" as they inspire and empower their followers: leadership, politics, media, movies, CEO of corporations

Personifications

- Your favorite inspirational leaders
- Apollo
- Jesus Christ
- King Arthur

The Teacher

Archetype of Knowledge and Guidance

Alchemical Correlation	Astrological Association
Fire-dissolving	December Sagittarius

Mission/Purpose: To bring knowledge and awareness to the people; to mentor and inspire

Mental Traits

- A mind hungry for knowledge
- Resourceful
- Views life experiences as "lessons"
- An expansive mind; ability to synthesize complex and diverse principles
- Open-minded to other perspectives although firm in their own beliefs
- Independent thinker: prefers gaining knowledge through own experiences
- A competitive mind; mentally sharp
- Ability to process information (and teach) through multiple intelligences
- Enjoys travel to broaden the mind

Emotional Expression

- Emotions often triggered by thoughts
- Passionate about a principle
- Emotions can intensify and become big when pursuing their visionary ideas and dreams
- Enthusiastic about what they know and wish to share with others
- Enjoys intimacy that includes freedom to adventure and travel

Physical Aspects

- Body correlations: hips, thighs, butt, liver (biggest internal organ)
- Athletic as a youth; team sports-oriented; the jock
- Medical problems may include: obesity, hip bursitis, liver cirrhosis
- Can become big (butt, hips . . .); as adults they often prefer to watch sports rather than play them; or read/lecture rather than remain active physically
- Sex for enjoyment, love, and adventure

Spiritual Tendencies

- Sense of connection to Divine through discussion of spiritual beliefs philosophically with the group or community
- Relates to mono- or polytheistic religions
- A sacred dialectic "high"

Shadow Characteristics

- Preachy; self-righteous
- The perpetual student (who won't teach) but is critical of teachers
- Loud, obnoxious; instigator
- Skeptic; argumentative without considering others

Interests/Involvements

Teaching, instructing, and mentorship: education, travel, adventure, research and writing, counseling, coaching, training

Personifications

- Your favorite teacher, mentor, or inspirational speaker
- Socrates
- The Sage or Prophet

The Nourisher

Archetype of Community and Nurturance

Alchemical Correlation	Astrological Association
Water-originating Water-creating	July Cancer

Mission/Purpose: To provide a sense of community, family, and home; to provide care for others

Mental Traits

- Conceptual thinking
- When asked, "What do you think?," replies: "I feel . . . "
- Relationship-oriented mind-set
- Considers patterns and themes rather than focus on facts and details

Emotional Expression

- Is comfortable with expressing full range of emotions and dealing with others' emotions
- Focus on nurturing and providing care
- Emotions are primary function and area of strength
- Unconditional love and compassion

Physical Aspects

- Body correlations: breasts, belly/stomach
- Round full bodies; voluptuous
- Sex for procreation or to comfort
- Medical problems may include: breast cancer, ulcers, stomach eating disorders including obesity, anorexia and bulimia

Spiritual Tendencies

- Spiritually intuitive through body wisdom
- Connects to Goddess traditions
- Earth as the Divine Mother in tribal cultures
- The Madonna/Mary, mother of God, is significant focus as Catholic example
- Theme of worship through Service

Shadow Characteristics

- Becomes the Martyr when taking care of others at expense of taking care of self
- Victim mentality
- Very cold and emotionless
- Selfish
- Refuses to be nourished; dislikes "touchy-feely" encounters
- "Mother issues" psychologically

Interests/Involvements

Community leaders, caregivers, homemakers, culinary arts focus, restaurant and food services, teachers (younger students), counselors, service-oriented professions

Personifications

- Betty Crocker
- Santa Claus
- The Great Mother figure

The Descender

Archetype of Transformation

Alchemical Correlation	Astrological Association
Water-maintaining	November Scorpio

Mission/Purpose: To honor the descent process and embrace transformation of Self

Mental Traits

- Focus on the deeper meaning of thoughts and ideas
- Conversations about death and taboo subjects
- Private and reflective
- Holds secrets
- Mysterious

Emotional Expression

- Primal expression of emotions
- Intense
- Emotionally resilient; willingness to move through challenges and difficult/ dark times as part of life for maturing
- Passionate
- Embraces Infinite compassion and everlasting torment as two poles of one energy

Physical Aspects

- Body correlations: genitals, anus, colon
- Sexuality is raw, passionate, embraces what may be considered taboo
- Medical problems may include sexually transmitted diseases, colon, prostate, cervical cancer, bipolar disorders, and depression

Spiritual Tendencies

- To commune deeply to the Creator, life must be offered; death leads to rebirth of the Soul
- Christianity theme of Jesus Christ's sacrifice for eternal salvation
- The Sundance ceremony of American Indians
- The Buddhist tenant: "life is suffering"
- Connection to the Divine through deep erotic expression

Shadow Characteristics

- Icy cold and cruel
- Control issues—fearful of losing control so try to control others and environment to an extreme
- Takes life, enjoys death; terrorizes

- Entitlement attitude that resents life challenges or dark moments
- Depression and extreme intensity—stuck in despair; bipolar; suicidal tendencies

Interests/Involvements

Positions that include working with death, dying, and deep transformation; in shadow, prostitutes: therapist, grief counselor, religious or spiritual group leader, hospice caregiver, surgeon and autopsy doctor, funeral director, military soldier, mercenary

Personifications

- Image of Jesus Christ bleeding on the cross
- Hades

- In wounded form, archetypal image of the Devil or the Dark Witch
- The Erotic Human

The Mystic Archetype of Cosmic Union	Alchemical Correlation	Astrological Association
	Water-dissolving	March Pisces

Mission/Purpose: To create soulful union with the Divine

Mental Traits

- Intuitive; not logical
- Psychic abilities

- Can appear distracted as thoughts wander
- Mental daydreams for problem solving

Emotional Expression

- Very empathetic; sensitive to the feelings of others
- The Urge to Merge— seeking that deep emotional connection with others

- Emotions may determine actions and behaviors

Physical Aspects

- Body correlations: feet and ankles; mental psychic abilities

- Medical problems: related to feet/ ankles and mental health issues

Spiritual Tendencies

- Connecting to the Creator through altered states
- Questing for Sacred Visions

- Focus on metaphysical spiritual practices such as going into trance or using dream work to channel God's messages

Shadow Characteristics

- Substance abuse and addictions
- Trust issues
- Aversion to altered states

- Codependency; extreme neediness in relationships

Interests/Involvements

Professions related to expanding the mind's abilities: podiatrist, reflexology, dance, mental health practitioners in fields of parapsychology and other alternative approaches that work with hypnotherapy, dreams, altered states due to breath work, etc.; magic

Personifications

- The Psychic Healer
- The Dancer
- Merlin the Magician